KIDDING Around ®

WASHINGTON, D.C.

WHAT TO DO, WHERE TO GO, AND HOW TO HAVE FUN IN WASHINGTON, D.C.

SECOND EDITION

by Debbie Levy

John Muir Publications
A Division of Avalon Travel Publishing

John Muir Publications
A Division of Avalon Travel Publishing
5855 Beaudry Street
Emeryville, CA 94608

Printed in the United States of America.
Second edition. First printing March 2000.

ISBN 1-56261-588-2

Editors Ellen Cavalli, Kristin Shahane
Production Janine Lehmann
Graphics Jane Susan MacCarter
Activities Kristin Shahane, Bobi Martin
Cover Design Caroline Van Remortel
Cover Photo Washington Stock Photos
Back Cover Photo Claude Moore Colonial Park
Illustrations Stacy Venturi-Pickett
Maps Susan Harrison
Printer Publishers Press

Distributed to the book trade by
Publishers Group West
Berkeley, California

CONTENTS

COLOR THE ROUTE
FROM YOUR HOMETOWN TO
WASHINGTON, D.C.

If you're flying, color the states you'll fly over. If you're driving, color the states you'll drive through. If you live in Washington, D.C., color the states you have traveled to.

WELCOME TO WASHINGTON, D.C.!

SOMEHOW IT ALL LOOKS FAMILIAR. YOU'VE SEEN the Capitol and the Washington Monument before— on television and in books. You've examined the Lincoln Memorial on the back of a $5 bill. You even know the name of the person who lives in the White House. But nothing compares to visiting the nation's capital in person. As you'll soon see, there's a lot more to Washington, D.C., than famous buildings. From hands-on museums to miles of hiking trails to one of the best zoos in the world, it's a capital city for kids.

⬆ **A view from high above the nation's capital**

HOW TO USE THIS BOOK

There's no wrong way to use this book. Skip around or read it straight through. Use the Contents page to see what the chapters cover or flip the pages to find an activity that catches your interest.

What month are you coming to Washington, D.C.? Check out the Calendar section to see what's happening then. Is there something special you want to see? Use the Index at the back of the book to find it. The Geographical Index will show you other cool things located in the same area. The Resource Guide has addresses you can write to for maps and other fun stuff. It also tells you what's open when and important telephone numbers.

A CAPITAL SPELLING LESSON

A capital is a town or city that serves as the seat of government. A capitol is a building where a law-making group, called a legislature, meets. The Capitol is the U.S. capitol, located in Washington, D.C., the U.S. capital.

You probably know that Washington, D.C., is named for the first president, George Washington. "D.C." stands for District of Columbia. The District, as it's called by locals, is not a part of any state, nor is it a state itself.

⚑ Take a tour of the White House and see where the president lives.

If you had a chance to rename the city of Washington, D.C., what would you want to call it? Why? Write your new name in the space provided.

DO THE WRITE THING

If you can, write a letter to your U.S. senator or representative several months before your visit. Ask for special tickets for VIP (very important person) tours of the White House and the Federal Bureau of Investigation (the FBI). These VIP tours, which must be arranged in advance, save you time waiting in lines. The VIP White House tour also includes more sights than the regular tours. You may also request passes to observe the House of Representatives or Senate when they are in session, and tickets for VIP tours of the Capitol, Supreme Court, Bureau of Engraving and Printing, and Kennedy Center. Be sure to mention when you'll be in town. Address your letter to your senator at: U.S. Senate, Washington, D.C. 20510. Send mail to your representative at: U.S. House of Representatives, Washington, D.C. 20515.

BIRTH OF A CAPITAL

Washington was the nation's third capital, after New York City and Philadelphia, but it was the first one to be built from the ground up. The U.S. Constitution directed Congress to create a "District" that would become "the Seat of the Government of the United States." The Constitution was very exact about some things concerning the federal district. For example, it was to be no larger than a square with sides of 10 miles each. But the big question was, where would the seat of government be located?

After years of argument, Congress decided the capital should be located on the Potomac River. In 1790, President George Washington scouted sites along the water and chose the area around the port of Georgetown, then a part of Maryland. The land close to the river was swampy and difficult to build on. Some farms and woods were further inland. There were no government buildings and no houses for the president and other officials. Everything would have to be built from scratch.

⚶ **Washington in its early days as a city**

Algonquin Indians and their ancestors used to live in the area now known as Washington. They left soon after the first Europeans traveled up the Potomac River in 1608.

BUILDING A CITY

After President Washington selected the site for the capital, work began on the Capitol building and the president's house, but it was slow going. When the government moved to Washington in 1800, only a few government buildings were partly built. The word to describe Washington in those days was "wet." How wet? Well, as you're strolling down Constitution Avenue, which stretches from the Lincoln Memorial up to Capitol Hill, be grateful your feet aren't stuck in muck.

Constitution Avenue used to be the Tiber Creek Canal. The canal was supposed to be a handy way to get around the city by boat. Instead, it became a filthy health hazard humming with mosquitoes. Even after city officials gave up on the Tiber Creek Canal, soggy ground continued to be a problem. The Washington Monument couldn't be built where it was planned because the land was too soft. Other government buildings have special supports that keep them from sinking into the soft earth.

⬆ A sketch of the Washington Monument being built

Washington, D.C., started out as a diamond. North of the Potomac River, the diamond was carved out of Maryland. The other half came from Virginia, but Virginians took back their half of the city in 1846.

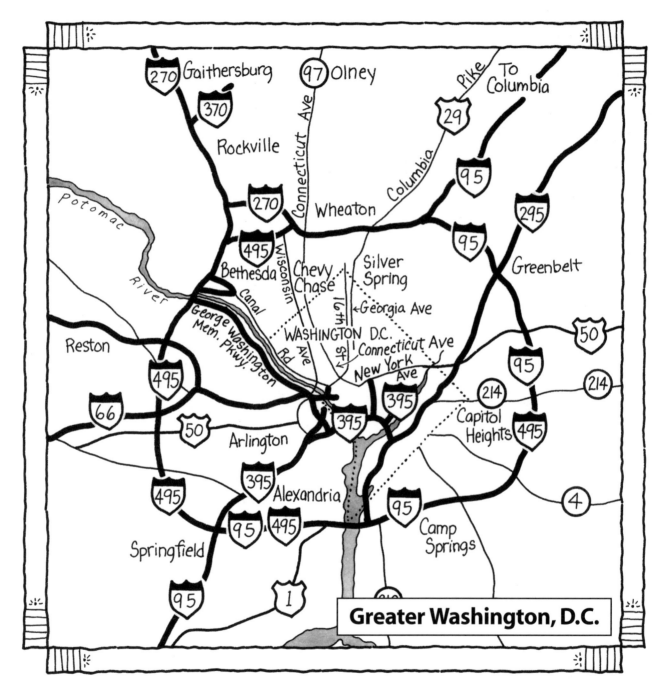

Greater Washington, D.C.

⇓ **Thousands of trees make Washington seem like one big park.**

WASHINGTON GROWS UP

Despite many obstacles, slowly but surely Washington grew into the visitor-friendly metropolis it is today. Around 519,000 people live in the city. The summers are as hot and damp as they ever were, but marshlands have been turned into playlands such as Constitution Gardens, and East and West Potomac Parks. Tens of thousands of trees make the city a green and shady space, ideal for walking around. And Washington is one of the only cities of its size with a clear view of the sky from downtown streets. Look up and you see sky, not skyscrapers. It's the law: no downtown building can rise above the top of the Capitol dome. But that doesn't count for the Washington Monument, the tallest structure in Washington.

WHAT'S THE WEATHER?

July is the hottest month; January is the coldest. Winters are mostly mild, without too much snow, but a snowstorm can stop the city cold! It's usually warm from April through October. Summer and holidays are when most people visit Washington, but because there's so much to see and do, any time is a good time.

Washington has no heavy industry, which is one of the reasons it is so clean—there are no smokestacks blowing pollution into the air, and no factories dumping waste into the river.

COLORFUL CULTURES

As the capital of the United States, Washington is first and foremost an American city. But it's also rich in cultures from other nations. Many Washingtonians come from Africa, the Caribbean, Korea, China, and Latin America. The city's multicultural flavor can be seen in its different neighborhoods, like funky Adams-Morgan and colorful Chinatown. The city's strong African American traditions are visible not only in restaurants where you can get down-home Southern cooking, but also at Howard University, which is known as one of the world's leading black universities.

HOMETOWN GREATS

When people think of Washingtonians, they think of politicians, but Washington has also produced many famous artists, writers, athletes, and entertainers.

⇡ **People from many different cultures live in D.C.**

World-class opera singer Denyce Graves started out singing in a D.C. church choir. Country singer Mary Chapin Carpenter calls Washington home. Popular R&B singer Roberta Flack grew up here. Olympic gold medalists Tom Dolan and Dominique Dawes both come from the suburbs. Actor Warren Beatty went to high school in nearby Arlington, Virginia. Jordan's Queen Noor was also a local. Perhaps the most famous homegrown "Washingtonian" isn't a person but a company: Northern Virginia's America Online.

Downtown Washington, D. C.

CITY LAYOUT

President George Washington selected French Major Pierre L'Enfant to plan the capital city. L'Enfant must have been a great geometry student; he created a city full of squares, circles, and rectangles. As you make your way around town, keep in mind that the city is laid out like a bunch of tic-tac-toe games stuck together. Streets that run north and south are numbered—First Street, Second Street, and so on. Streets that run east and west are named for the letters of the alphabet up to W Street (but there's no J Street). Plus, the city is divided into four sections: northwest, northeast, southwest, southeast. On top of all this, avenues run on a diagonal and they're named for the states that existed at the time the city was planned. When a diagonal meets a letter street and a number street at the same time, that's where you'll find one of L'Enfant's circles, which drive today's drivers crazy! Many of the city's most popular museums and memorials are built around the National Mall, a 2-mile grassy rectangle that goes from Capitol Hill to the Lincoln Memorial.

⬆ There is a lot to explore in Washington's museums.

At Freedom Plaza near the White House, you can study L'Enfant's design on the giant map of Washington etched in granite.

WHAT DOESN'T BELONG?

This is a scene that might have existed in Washington, D.C., 150 years ago. But you'll notice many things that didn't exist back then. When you find something that doesn't belong, circle it. Then color in the scene. Hint: There are at least 12 things that don't belong.

TRAVEL TIPS

The best way to get around, especially when visiting the major sights around the National Mall, is to walk. When you get tired, consider hailing a cab. You might also find Metrobus convenient. Several tour buses also operate in the city, many of which let you get off and on throughout the day so you can see the sights at your own pace.

For trips off the Mall, take the subway, which everyone calls the Metro. You can go all around town and to nearby Maryland and Virginia by Metro. Make sure you check a map before you board a train because Metro station names can be misleading—for example the Capitol South stop is blocks away from the Capitol.

Here are some ideas of what to take when you're out exploring Washington, D.C.!

WORKING WASHINGTON

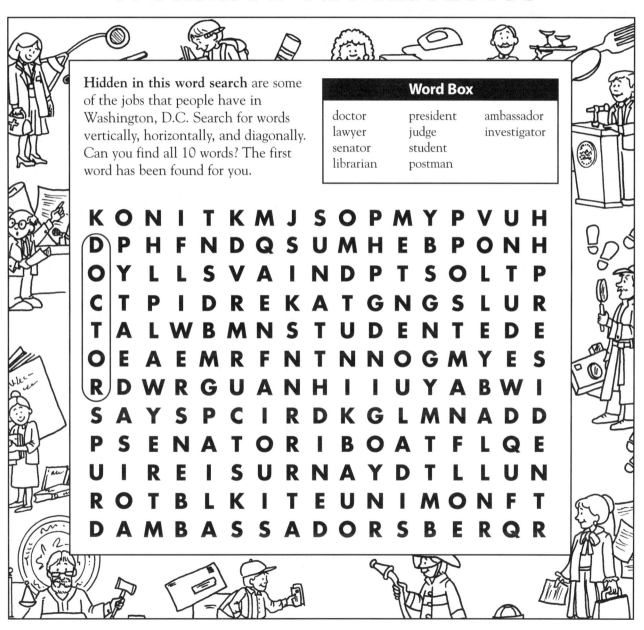

Hidden in this word search are some of the jobs that people have in Washington, D.C. Search for words vertically, horizontally, and diagonally. Can you find all 10 words? The first word has been found for you.

Word Box		
doctor	president	ambassador
lawyer	judge	investigator
senator	student	
librarian	postman	

```
K O N I T K M J S O P M Y P V U H
D P H F N D Q S U M H E B P O N H
O Y L L S V A I N D P T S O L T P
C T P I D R E K A T G N G S L U R
T A L W B M N S T U D E N T E D E
O E A E M R F N T N N O G M Y E S
R D W R G U A N H I I U Y A B W I
S A Y S P C I R D K G L M N A D D
P S E N A T O R I B O A T F L Q E
U I R E I S U R N A Y D T L L U N
R O T B L K I T E U N I M O N F T
D A M B A S S A D O R S B E R Q R
```

2 PARKS AND THE GREAT OUTDOORS

THE NATION'S CAPITAL HAS OUTDOOR places to suit all kinds of outdoor enthusiasts. For those who like their spaces unfenced and untamed, the perfect place may be Rock Creek Park. When you're hiking through its acres of forests, the city feels far away although it's really all around you. For those who seek spectacular sights, Great Falls offers wild waterfalls over a rocky river bed. For the history-minded, a visit to one of Washington's Civil War forts, or a barge ride on the old Chesapeake and Ohio Canal, provides fresh air and a taste of old times.

⇑ **The wild and rocky waterfalls at Great Falls Park**

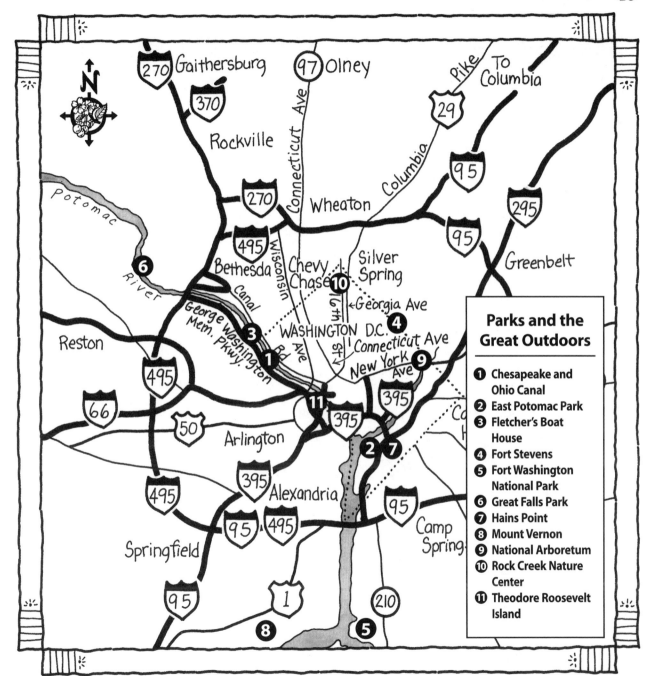

Parks and the Great Outdoors

1. Chesapeake and Ohio Canal
2. East Potomac Park
3. Fletcher's Boat House
4. Fort Stevens
5. Fort Washington National Park
6. Great Falls Park
7. Hains Point
8. Mount Vernon
9. National Arboretum
10. Rock Creek Nature Center
11. Theodore Roosevelt Island

ROCK CREEK PARK

You'll find plenty of room to stretch your legs here. Rock Creek Park was the first city park ever founded by Congress. Although created back in 1890, today it is still one of the largest city parks in the United States. Within Washington, Rock Creek Park has 29 miles of hiking trails, 11 miles of bridle paths for horseback riding, and a bike route that runs from the Lincoln Memorial to Maryland.

Start your explorations at the **Rock Creek Nature Center and Planetarium**. Here you can go on a guided nature walk, and the planetarium offers astronomy programs especially for kids. Nearby, **Rock Creek Gallery** houses exhibits by local artists, and **Peirce Mill**, a gristmill from the early 1800s, is a step back in time. You can arrange pony and horse rides at the **Rock Creek Horse Center**.

The Native Americans who used to live along Rock Creek used stones from the creek to make tools and weapons.

⇡ **A guide talks to a group at Rock Creek Nature Center before a nature walk.**

ROCK CREEK RAMBLE

Holly the horseback rider needs to get some hay for her horse Hank. Can you help them get to Rock Creek Horse Center?

CHESAPEAKE AND OHIO CANAL

The C&O Canal, as it's known, was built alongside the Potomac River in the early 1800s. It served as a water highway to bring coal to the capital on barges from the mountains of Maryland. Children often drove the mules that pulled the barges.

The **Canal Towpath** is a wonderful place to hike, bike, walk, and run. You could start in the city near **Fletcher's Boat House** and walk 15 miles to Great Falls, Maryland. From there you could hike on a trail all the way to Georgia without ever leaving the woods!

For shorter walks, stroll the Towpath in D.C.'s Georgetown neighborhood. If weather and canal conditions permit, you can take a mule-drawn barge ride on the canal. National Park Service guides dress in nineteenth-century costumes and, for an hour and a half, tell you about life on the canal in the 1800s.

Mules used to pull barges on the C&O Canal in the 1800s.

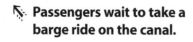

Passengers wait to take a barge ride on the canal.

HIDE AND SEEK!

Can you find the hidden objects in this picture? When you find one, draw a circle around it. When you're done, color the scene. Look for: screwdriver, paintbrush, loaf of bread, hot dog, goblet, sucker, pencil, suitcase, guitar, comb, face, sunglasses, scissors, mouse.

GREAT FALLS PARK

There are two parks at the Potomac River's Great Falls, one on the Maryland side of the river and the other on the Virginia side. Both offer fantastic views of the rocky waterfalls that drop a total of 76 feet through Mather Gorge. Upstream and downstream from the falls the river looks calm, but it's not. Currents can easily pull a good swimmer under 50 feet of water. No swimming allowed!

On the Maryland side, you can walk the C&O Canal Towpath. If you're good on your feet, try the **Billy Goat Trail**, a rocky 4-mile hike between the canal and the river. Before you leave, visit **Great Falls Tavern and Museum,** which was originally a stop on the canal route.

Over in Virginia, the park offers excellent hiking trails and the best views of the falls. Wave to the people you see across the river in Maryland!

Some of the best kayakers in the country, including members of U.S. Olympic teams, practice their moves in the dangerous waters at Great Falls. Look for them in the river during your visit.

⇧ **A brave kayaker takes on the Potomac River.**

THE DAY THE FALLS DIDN'T FALL

Without telling anyone what you're doing, ask for a word to fill in each blank. For example, "Give me an action word." When all the blanks are filled in, read the story out loud. One of the blanks has been filled in for you.

One day long ago a _____ fairy flew over the Great Falls. "I'm tired,"
describing word

yawned the fairy. "I need a ___**nap**___." He lay down on the grass.
thing

But the sound of the Great Falls was too _____. He took out his
describing word

magic _____ and _____ed it over the falls. Instantly, the water
thing   action word

stopped. _____ hours later, the fairy woke up. Some children were
number

_____ing at the falls. "What happened to the water?"
action word

asked one. "_____!" cried the fairy. Quickly he waved his wand
exclamation

and the falls started _____ing.
action word

THEODORE ROOSEVELT ISLAND

This Potomac River island is only 10 minutes from downtown, but it feels like it's worlds away. Throughout the thick forest, swamp, and rocks you may see rabbits, beavers, hawks, turtles, and frogs. The island is wild, but it's not too big so you can really explore. Wear your oldest shoes for mucking around in swampland. Set out on the **Swamp Trail**, where you're likely to run into ducks and geese. Cut the chatter as you approach the river so you don't scare away the great blue heron. If you're lucky, you may see one fishing in the river.

Besides the wildlife, the island has a large statue of Theodore Roosevelt, the outdoorsman and twenty-sixth president. He believed in conservation and preserving the environment years before everyone else began talking about those issues.

T.R., as President Roosevelt was known, created the U.S. Forest Service, 51 bird sanctuaries, and five national parks.

⇐ **Theodore Roosevelt Island**

FIND THE TURTLES

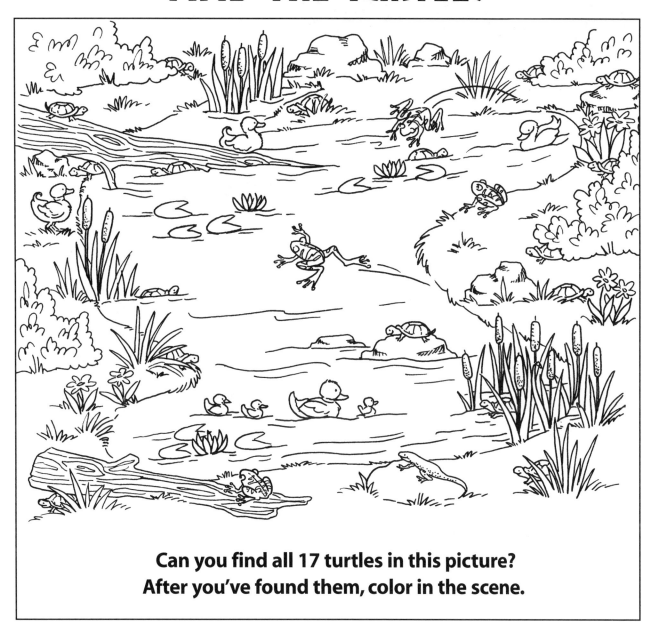

**Can you find all 17 turtles in this picture?
After you've found them, color in the scene.**

HAINS POINT

Everyone can find something to enjoy at Hains Point. This park is at the tip of a long tongue of land called **East Potomac Park**. You can walk along the Potomac River on a 5-mile path. Eat a picnic, play on a playground, swim in a pool, and watch airplanes take off from Washington National Airport. You can even play miniature golf, and tennis courts and ball fields round out the attractions.

If all the activity makes you sleepy, *The Awakening* will wake you up. It's a giant, touchable sculpture by J. Seward Johnson of a bearded man half-buried in the ground—and he's trying to get out! His head is visible, as are his 17-foot-long right arm and shoulder, and part of his left hand.

⬆ *The Awakening,* the eye-opening sculpture in East Potomac Park

A DAY AT THE PARK

Hidden in this word search are some things you might see or do in a Washington, D.C., park. Search for words vertically, horizontally, and diagonally. Can you find all 12 words? The first word has been found for you.

Word Box

birds	trees	swings
picnic	run	hike
ponds	tennis courts	fish
bike path	skate	sculpture

```
R O T A T H I K E O P S W I N G S
H P C E R D Q S Y M H E S A O N H
G W G L N G A I N N T T C B L T F
P T S O D N S K A A I N U F L U D
R O A W G M I R K V C E L T I D N
S F N E M D F S G N N O P T Y S Y
P D S D G U N N C U I U T E B W H
I A X S S C I N D O C L U R A D W
C Y B I K E P A T H U A R U N Q T
N I A R T S D L N P Y R E M O I B
I O T B B I R D S U L I T R E E S
C P D N I O P Y F K J Z H S E Q R
```

NATIONAL ARBORETUM

**Very old (but very small)
⇣ bonsai trees**

If you enjoy nature and woods but can't tell a myrtle bush from a magnolia, this the place for you. Here, on 444 hilly acres, the plants wear name tags. The arboretum is a huge government garden that does research on trees and shrubs that grow in the United States. It's also a wonderful place to bike (on 10 miles of paved paths), or hike on footpaths at your own pace.

Bonsai trees can be very expensive. The arboretum's bonsai are worth more than $4 million. No wonder they're kept in their own special building!

Perhaps the most amazing thing to see at the arboretum is the **National Bonsai and Penjing Museum**. Bonsai is the Japanese art of growing miniature trees in small shallow pots. In China, it's called *penjing*. The trees are trained by the bonsai artist to grow into decorative and unusual shapes. At the arboretum, some of these strange little trees are more than 300 years old—yet they are no more than 2 feet high!

**The National Bonsai ⇗
and Penjing Museum**

WHICH ARE THE SAME?

Can you tell which two bonsai trees in the arboretum are exactly alike? When you've circled the trees that are the same, color in the scene.

MOUNT VERNON

George Washington was the only president who never lived in the White House. When he was president he lived in New York and Philadelphia.

But the first president's real home was an 8,000-acre Virginia plantation known as Mount Vernon. Mount Vernon is a short drive, bus ride, boat trip, or bicycle journey away from downtown D.C. Besides the mansion and outbuildings, you can explore the Mount Vernon Forest Trail, which leads to the **George Washington: Pioneer Farmer** site. This area features the **16-Sided Barn**, where horses "tread" or stomp on wheat to separate the grain from the straw. If you feel like trying your hand at old-fashioned farming, the Pioneer Farmer site has jobs for people, too!

Mount Vernon also offers a walking tour of slave life on the estate (George Washington was a slave-owner). During the summer months, be sure to visit the **Hands-On-History** area, where you might play corncob darts, spin wool, or construct a bucket.

⇧ **The gardens at Mount Vernon**

The Spirit Cruise runs round-trip boat rides down the Potomac from D.C. to the Mount Vernon wharf, and includes time to tour the plantation. You can also take a shorter ride on the Potomac River at Mount Vernon—a great opportunity to take photos.

PIONEERING SPIRIT

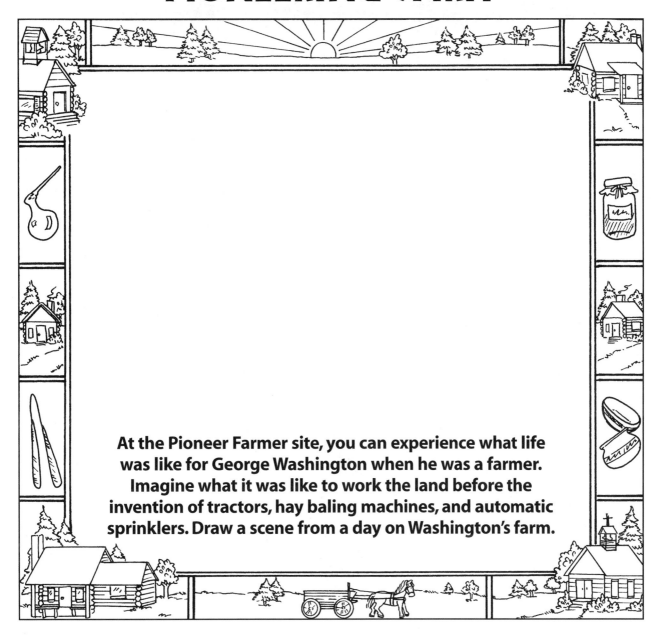

At the Pioneer Farmer site, you can experience what life was like for George Washington when he was a farmer. Imagine what it was like to work the land before the invention of tractors, hay baling machines, and automatic sprinklers. Draw a scene from a day on Washington's farm.

FORT WASHINGTON NATIONAL PARK

Step inside this gigantic fort and you step back in time. Fort Washington was considered important in defending the capital during the Civil War, but it never actually came under attack. With 46-foot-high walls, a wooden drawbridge, moat, and 85 cannon stations, Fort Washington has lots to explore. Take a look at the fort's dark, dank jail and you'll be on your best behavior.

Sixty-eight forts once formed a ring around Washington during the Civil War. Most are in ruins today, but some are fun to visit. At **Fort Stevens** you can see where the city came under attack during the Civil War by 20,000 Confederate soldiers. President Abraham Lincoln came to the fort during the battle, making him the only president to withstand enemy fire while in office.

⬆ **A Civil War cannon at Fort Washington**

MY TRAVEL JOURNAL
—Parks and the Great Outdoors—

I had fun when I visited: _____

I learned about: _____

My favorite park was: _____

This is a picture of what I saw at a park in Washington, D.C.

3 ANIMALS AROUND WASHINGTON, D.C.

IN WASHINGTON'S EARLY DAYS, THE MOST talked-about animals were the snakes and insects that crawled around in the swampy lowlands. Today there are many more interesting animals to talk about. You can join orangutans in their special classroom at the National Zoo's Think Tank, watch how quickly the National Aquarium's piranhas gobble up their lunch, or walk among the frogs and turtles at Kenilworth Aquatic Gardens. Yes, you can still see (and touch) snakes and insects, but happily they won't be slithering underfoot or swarming overhead. They'll be in their homes at the National Zoo.

↥ **A tiger swallowtail butterfly on a lily at Kenilworth Aquatic Gardens**

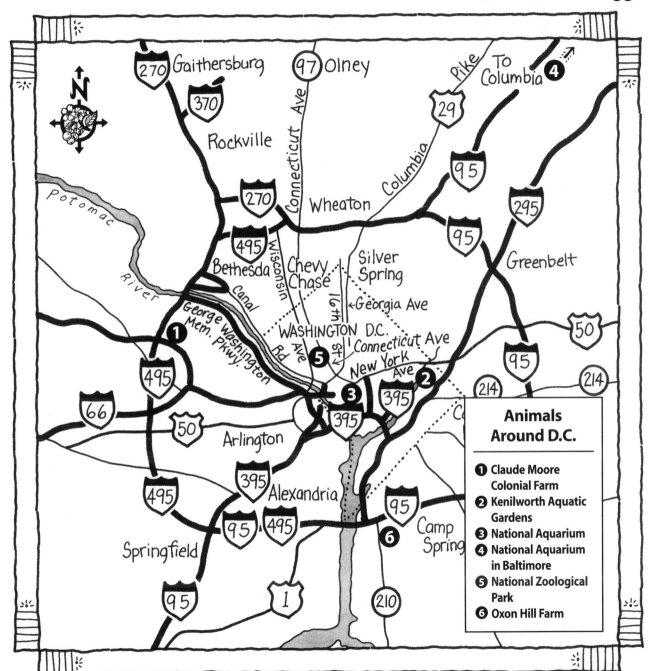

Animals
Around D.C.

❶ Claude Moore
Colonial Farm
❷ Kenilworth Aquatic
Gardens
❸ National Aquarium
❹ National Aquarium
in Baltimore
❺ National Zoological
Park
❻ Oxon Hill Farm

NATIONAL ZOOLOGICAL PARK

Lions and tigers and bears . . . oh my! The zoo is home to more than 5,800 animals, and you can get up close and personal with many of them. Have an inside view of a lion's life in the sprawling **Great Cats** exhibit, which includes the Great Cats trail and **Tiger Tracks**, an interactive introduction to the world of tigers. At the **American Prairies** exhibit, you'll see bison and prairie dogs in their natural grasslands surroundings. Listen to the prairie dogs talking and singing—they are actually communicating with each other when they make those noises.

Some of the zoo's animals put on shows for visitors. At the **Sea Lion Pool**, watch the sea lions frolic during their daily performance. The elephants may not be as acrobatic as they go through their exercises in the **Elephant Yard**, but they'll show you some surprising moves, too. At the **Cheetah Conservation Station**, you may catch a cheetah speeding by, faster than a car on the highway.

⬆ **Get up close and personal with this lion at the National Zoological Park.**

Don't be embarrassed when you see the prairie dogs kiss one another. Pressing their teeth together is how they recognize each other.

WHAT'S WRONG HERE?

It's a strange day at the zoo and lots of things are out of place.
Find at least 12 things that you think are wrong in this picture.
Circle them when you find them and then color the scene.

INDOORS AT THE ZOO

A rainy day is still a fine day to visit the National Zoological Park, because many of its most fascinating attractions are indoors. **The Invertebrate Exhibit** is a building for animals without backbones. Pet a giant Madagascar cockroach, stare down a scorpion, or scope out the arthropods under a microscope. In the nearby **Pollinarium**, you can see a beehive as large as a picture window, and watch as the bees build their hive. The **Amazonia** exhibit re-creates a tropical rain forest, teeming with exotic wildlife, including giant river fish, monkeys, and birds.

To see radical reptiles, go to the **Reptile Discovery Center**. There you'll find super-sized snakes and the largest species of lizard in the world, the Komodo dragon. And if you think your pet is smart, you won't want to miss the **Think Tank**. Watch the orangutans communicate with people, using symbols instead of words. Then play games that demonstrate your own power of thinking.

An alligator smiles for the camera.

In the wild, Komodo dragons eat whole deer and pigs. At the Reptile Discovery Center, they feast once a week on dead rats, rabbits, and chickens.

MYSTERY AT THE ZOO

Without telling anyone what you're doing, ask for a word to fill in each blank. For example, "Give me an action word." When all the blanks are filled in, read the story out loud. One of the blanks has been filled in for you.

Mr. _____ the zoo keeper was _____. He was sure he
       name 1   emotion

had locked the _____ in the _____ where he stored the
            thing   place

chimpanzee's bag of peanuts. But the bag was gone! _____ing
                                         action word

around, he saw a trail of _____. He followed the trail to the
                       things

chimpanzee's _____. The happy chimp was _____ing
             place   action word

the peanuts. "_____!" said Mr. _____. "How did you get
            exclamation   name 1

those?" He took the bag and put it away. The __sneaky___
                                        describing word

chimpanzee wasn't worried. After all, he had the zoo keeper's keys!

ANIMAL FARMS

Travel back in time (but only a short distance from downtown D.C.) to the **Claude Moore Colonial Farm** in McLean, Virginia. The tools, farming methods, and clothes worn by this farm's "family" are all true to the 1770s. Hogs, chickens, dairy cows, and turkeys roam around, just as they did back then. There are pigs to feed, butter to churn, fish to preserve, and fields to weed. With all that work to be done, you're sure to find a job that's fun and helpful.

Another place with lovable livestock is **Oxon Hill Farm**, where you can experience life on a farm in the early 1900s. Farm workers might be shearing sheep, milking cows, feeding chickens, or pressing apples for cider. They can use your help, so lend a hand!

⇞ **Helping out at Claude Moore Colonial Farm**

⇞ **Enjoy a wagon ride at Oxon Hill Farm.**

For plenty of prize-winning farm animals—and for entertainment, food, and carnival rides—visit an agricultural fair in the countryside surrounding the capital. Late summer is the "hottest" season for fairs, when lots of them take place in nearby Maryland and Virginia.

CROSSWORD FUN

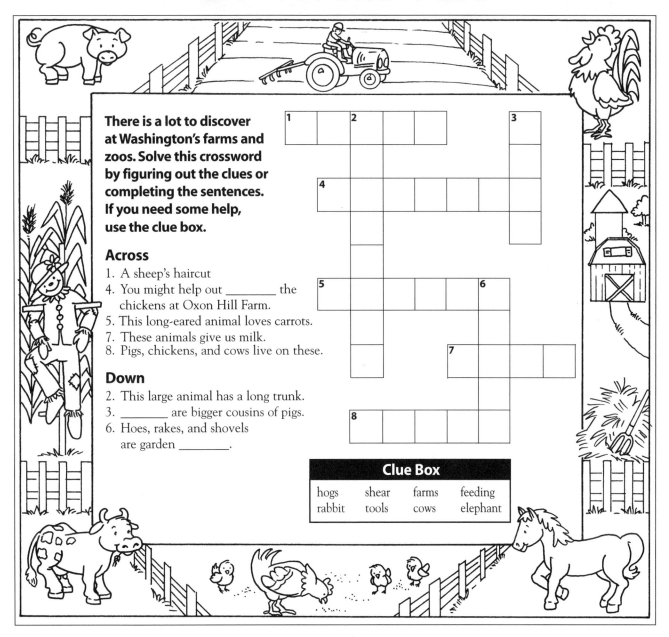

There is a lot to discover at Washington's farms and zoos. Solve this crossword by figuring out the clues or completing the sentences. If you need some help, use the clue box.

Across

1. A sheep's haircut
4. You might help out _____ the chickens at Oxon Hill Farm.
5. This long-eared animal loves carrots.
7. These animals give us milk.
8. Pigs, chickens, and cows live on these.

Down

2. This large animal has a long trunk.
3. _____ are bigger cousins of pigs.
6. Hoes, rakes, and shovels are garden _____.

Clue Box

hogs	shear	farms	feeding
rabbit	tools	cows	elephant

THE NATIONAL AQUARIUM

This is the oldest public aquarium in the United States, but its fish are definitely young at heart, especially at feeding time. If you think someone you know has bad table manners, take a look at the meat-eating piranhas and sharks as they fight to get their fill of lunch—shrimp, squid, smelts, and fish. Of course, these two species live in separate tanks so they won't chow down on each other.

If you're willing to put your hands in the water, visit the **Touch Tank**. There you can play with a horseshoe crab, a starfish, or a sea urchin. Then stroll around and examine more than 1,500 wet pets, including baby alligators, sea turtles, moray eels, and colorful Japanese carp, called koi.

When the National Aquarium's electric eel has something to say, he doesn't talk—he buzzes with electricity. The eel's electricity activates special sensors in the tank that cause the buzzing sound.

↑ **Dip your hand in the Touch Tank at the National Aquarium.**

WHAT'S THE DIFFERENCE?

These two pictures of an aquarium might look the same, but they are not. How many differences between the two scenes can you find? Hint: There are at least 12 differences.

THE NATIONAL AQUARIUM IN BALTIMORE

Only a 30-minute train ride or 50-minute car ride from downtown D.C., Baltimore's National Aquarium has five levels of exhibits. Along with thousands of fabulous fish in the main building, there's a separate 1.2-million-gallon **Marine Mammal Pavilion**, where bottlenose dolphins put on daily shows. Seals live in a free outdoor exhibit, where you can watch their feedings and training sessions.

At the **Open Ocean Exhibit**, get eye-to-eye with sharks. The 335,000-gallon **Atlantic Coral Reef Exhibit** also makes you feel as if you're underwater. Watch divers as they feed the fishes, rays, and other sea creatures.

Wings in the Water features the largest collection of sting rays in the United States. At the **Children's Cove**, you can touch sea animals like sea stars and crabs. Finally, for a different water world, the **South American Rain Forest** is where you'll find interesting creatures like poison dart frogs and piranhas.

⇑ **Dolphins (and their trainer!) leap and splash during their daily shows.**

⇑ **Holding a crab at Children's Cove**

WHERE ARE THE SEA STARS?

Can you find all 17 sea stars in this picture?
After you find them, color the scene.

KENILWORTH AQUATIC GARDENS

Shy animals at Kenilworth Gardens have plenty of good places to hide, like under the Amazon water lily's 6-foot leaves!

Countless wetland animals make their homes in or around the 44 ponds and a 2-mile trail in this restored marsh. Look out for bullfrogs and leopard frogs, snapping turtles, and spadefoot toads at this 14-acre park. You may also see water snakes, mud minnows, sunfish, dragonflies, and beetles. In warm weather, the gardens attract a lot of butterflies. Most thrilling of all, you could spot a migrating bald eagle or great blue heron.

This is the only national park devoted entirely to water plants—more than 100,000 of them. Flowering lotuses, lilies, and bamboo grow in or on the ponds and marshes. Some types of lotus plants are 6 feet tall, with blossoms larger than soccer balls. It's best to visit in the morning or early afternoon, since many of the blooms close in the heat of the afternoon.

← The marshlands at Kenilworth are home to many wetland plants and animals.

⬆ Boys holding snakes at Kenilworth's visitor center

MY TRAVEL JOURNAL

—Animals around Washington, D.C.—

I had fun when I visited: _____

My favorite animal was: _____

What I enjoyed doing the most was: _____

This is a picture of an animal I saw

4 LANDMARKS AND MONUMENTS

WASHINGTON IS A CITY OF MONUMENTS and landmarks, many of which you've probably seen in books or on television. You'll want to visit the famous ones, like the Capitol and the White House. For a special treat, go on a moonlight tour of the four major presidential monuments—the Washington, the Lincoln, the Jefferson, and the FDR. Even on a warm night you may feel shivers down your spine as you gaze up and think of what these nation-builders did for their country. But don't pass up the lesser-known landmarks. And if you think bigger is better, visit the Grant Memorial near the U.S. Capitol— it's the largest statue in Washington. It is dedicated to the Civil War hero and eighteenth president Ulysses S. Grant.

The Washington Monument is the tallest building in D.C.

Landmarks and Monuments

❶ **Constitution Gardens**
❷ **Emancipation Statue**
❸ **Ford's Theater and Petersen House**
❹ **FDR Memorial**
❺ **Jefferson Memorial**
❶ **The Korean War Veterans Memorial**
❻ **Lincoln Memorial**
❼ **The Supreme Court**
❽ **The U.S. Capitol and Grant Memorial**
❶ **The Vietnam Veterans Memorial**
❾ **Washington Monument**
❿ **The White House**

Logan Circle

Scott Circle

Thomas Circle

29

Mt. Vernon Square

Franklin Park

Vermont

Lafayette Square

New York

Massachusetts

❷

395

50

50

50

❸

D St

Pennsylvania Ave

WHITE HOUSE

❿

The Ellipse

15th St

17th

Washington Monument

Louisiana Ave

Constitution

50

1

50

Constitution

Ave

ALT 1

U.S. Capitol

❼

❽

❻ Lincoln Memorial

❶

ALT 50

Washington Monument

ALT 50

❾

THE MALL

St

ALT 50

Jefferson Dr

Independance

14th

L'Enfant Promenade

Maryland

Tidal Basin

Thomas Jefferson Memorial

❹

❺

C

4th St

3rd St

395

ALT 1

395

Canal St

Potomac River

Washington Channel

N

New Jersey Ave

Island Ave

Rhode

17th St

16th St

mont Circle

9th St

1

1

12th St

7th St

6th St

3rd St

1st St

U.S. CAPITOL

The high white dome of the U.S. Capitol is famous around the world as the symbol of Washington, D.C. This is where Congress meets to pass laws and approve treaties, or agreements. Free guided tours start in the **Rotunda**, underneath the 9-million-pound cast iron dome. Artist Constantino Brumidi worked on the dome's elaborate paintings for a year while lying on a platform 180 feet above the floor. In the **Visitor's Gallery**, you may watch Congress in session.

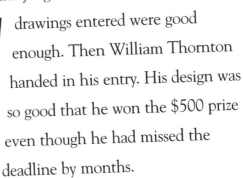

At the foot of the Capitol stands the U.S. Botanic Garden, where all kinds of strange and wonderful plants are grown. It's the oldest botanic garden in the United States.

The Capitol was built on a site personally selected by George Washington. A contest was held for the best building design, but the judges didn't think any of the 15 drawings entered were good enough. Then William Thornton handed in his entry. His design was so good that he won the $500 prize even though he had missed the deadline by months.

⬅ **The Capitol in winter**

HIDE AND SEEK!

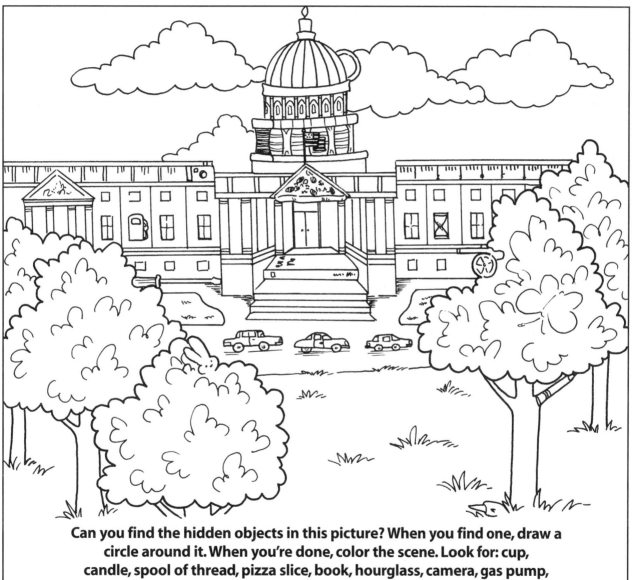

Can you find the hidden objects in this picture? When you find one, draw a circle around it. When you're done, color the scene. Look for: cup, candle, spool of thread, pizza slice, book, hourglass, camera, gas pump, butterfly, pencil, bunny face, ruler, bird head, screwdriver, cannon.

THE WHITE HOUSE

What house in Washington has 132 rooms, 32 bathrooms, and its own movie theater? It's the president's house—more commonly known as the White House. There are also 412 doors, three elevators, and seven staircases. The White House was the largest house in the United States until the Civil War. It has been the official home of the president of the United States and the first family since 1800.

Tours of the White House are available, but the public is shown only a few rooms, so don't expect to see the president or his family. You'll see the East Room, the largest room in the house. Today it's used for ceremonies and press conferences. In the past, however, it's been used as a bicycle track by President James Garfield's sons and as a wrestling arena by President Theodore Roosevelt!

The White House has been the home of many "first pets." These include Chelsea Clinton's cat, Socks; Caroline Kennedy's pony, Macaroni; and a goat named Old Whiskers that belonged to President Benjamin Harrison's son.

← **The White House, home of the president of the United States**

DESIGN THE PRESIDENTIAL SEAL

The Presidential Seal, pictured here, is the official symbol of the president of the United States.

The olive branch is a symbol of peace and the arrows are symbols of war. Before World War II, the eagle faced the arrows. After that war, President Harry Truman changed the seal so that the eagle now points toward the symbol of peace.

If you were designing the Presidential Seal, what symbols would you use to represent the U.S. and the president? Draw a new and improved Presidential Seal of your own design in the blank circle.

THE WASHINGTON MONUMENT

The first monument for President Washington was a large marble statue in which he is shown wrapped in a toga, naked from the waist up. It shocked Washingtonians of the 1800s and now sits in the Smithsonian's National Museum of American History.

So, the 555-foot tall obelisk (or pillar) on the Mall is actually the second monument created for the first president. It sways a little on windy days, but it won't tip over. The monument is secured by 15-foot-thick walls at the base, as well as a foundation that reaches 36 feet underground. There are 897 steps inside, but you aren't allowed to walk to the top. Instead, you ride the high-speed elevator, which whisks you up in 70 seconds.

The Washington Monument is two different colors because construction on the monument, which began in 1848, stopped in 1854 at 170 feet. When it resumed 25 years later, the marble came from a different level of the quarry. The newer marble has a slightly darker color.

←
The Washington Monument was covered with 32 miles of scaffolding during its 1998–2000 renovation.

MAKING A MONUMENT

Hidden in this word search are some items needed to build a monument. Search for words vertically, horizontally, and diagonally. Can you find all 12 words? The first word has been found for you.

Word Box

marble	trucks	tools
columns	scaffold	crane
brick	iron	steel
blueprints	glass	architect

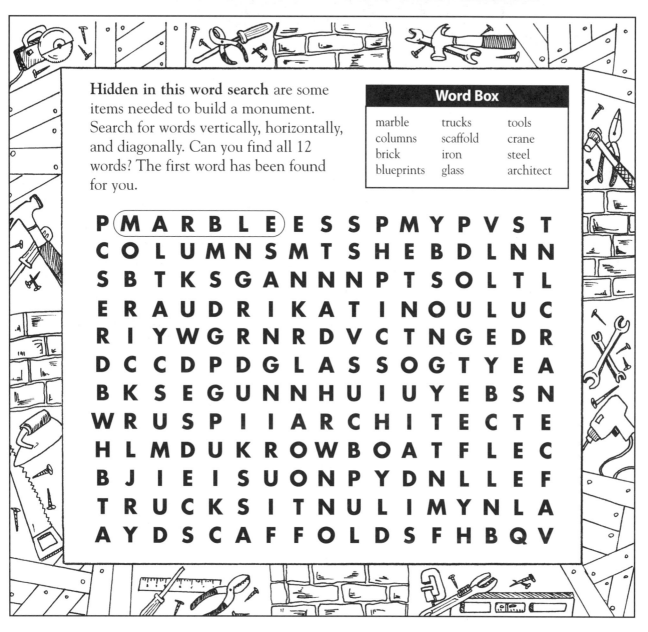

```
P M A R B L E E S S P M Y P V S T
C O L U M N S M T S H E B D L N N
S B T K S G A N N N P T S O L T L
E R A U D R I K A T I N O U L U C
R I Y W G R N R D V C T N G E D R
D C C D P D G L A S S O G T Y E A
B K S E G U N N H U I U Y E B S N
W R U S P I I A R C H I T E C T E
H L M D U K R O W B O A T F L E C
B J I E I S U O N P Y D N L L E F
T R U C K S I T N U L I M Y N L A
A Y D S C A F F O L D S F H B Q V
```

THE LINCOLN MEMORIAL

The Lincoln Memorial is a gigantic, dignified structure near the Potomac River. You have to climb 56 steps to enter it, one step for each year of Abraham Lincoln's life. The 36 outside columns stand for the 36 states that existed when Lincoln died. The statue of Lincoln, the sixteenth president, is made of 28 blocks of marble that fit together like a puzzle.

Lincoln looks thoughtful, almost sad, in the statue. He was president when the United States began its most serious crisis, the Civil War. He took action to end slavery in this country. He prevented the nation from dividing in two.

The Lincoln Memorial overlooks the Reflecting Pool. In 1963, nearly 250,000 people crowded around this area to hear Dr. Martin Luther King Jr. deliver his famous "I Have A Dream" speech.

⬆ **The Lincoln Memorial, with the Reflecting Pool and the Washington Monument in the background**

If the seated statue of Lincoln were to stand up, it would be 28 feet tall.

CROSSWORD FUN

There are a lot of interesting facts to discover about President Lincoln. Solve this crossword by figuring out the clues or completing the sentences. If you need some help, use the clue box.

Across

1. The leader of our country is called this.
4. Lincoln's first name
7. There are 56 steps leading to the memorial, the same number of years in Lincoln's _____.
8. Lincoln worked to end this in America.

Down

1. You can see one of these at Ford's Theater.
2. It took 28 blocks of marble to make the _____ of Lincoln.
3. Where Lincoln was shot or where you'd go to see a movie
5. Lincoln's wife's first name
6. The _____ War nearly split our country in two.

Clue Box

theater	Abraham
Mary	play
slavery	Civil
statue	president
life	

FORD'S THEATER AND PETERSEN HOUSE

You can get tickets to see a play at Ford's Theater, or you can skip the stage and go directly to the basement. There's plenty of historical drama down there in the **Lincoln Museum**. The museum tells the story of President Abraham Lincoln's assassination, which occured in this very theater. While watching a comedy on April 14, 1865, Lincoln was shot by John Wilkes Booth, an actor who had performed at the theater. The assassin's gun is on display in the museum.

⇑ **The booth at Ford's Theater where Lincoln was shot**

Across from Ford's Theater is Petersen House, where Lincoln died at 7:22 a.m. the morning after he was shot. You can see the bed where the president had to be placed diagonally because at 6 feet, 4 inches, he was longer than the mattress. Even the blood-stained pillow is still in place.

← **Petersen House**

COLOR THE SCENE

Ford's Theater has been restored to the way it appeared on the night Lincoln was shot. Color in the scene using whatever colors you like.

THE SUPREME COURT

Known as the highest court in the land, the Supreme Court decides some of the most important legal questions of the day. Every year the court is asked to decide 7,000 to 8,000 cases, but it agrees to take on only around 150. From October to April, you may see the court in session. Court sessions open with the loud knock of a gavel, or hammer, indicating that everyone must stand. Then the nine Supreme Court justices, wearing black robes, enter from behind their bench. Each side in a case gets half an hour to talk. At the end of that time, the lawyer who's arguing must stop talking, even if he or she hasn't finished.

There's a different sort of court above the library on the building's fourth floor—the Supreme Court basketball court. It's used by the justices, their clerks, and invited guests.

Olympic Dream Team member Charles Barkley dribbled and passed with Supreme Court Justice Clarence Thomas on the Supreme Court basketball court.

⇚ **The statue *Justice* greets visitors to the Supreme Court.**

⇓ **The Supreme Court**

A DAY IN COURT

Without telling anyone what you're doing, ask for a word to fill in each blank. For example, "Give me an action word." When all the blanks are filled in, read the story out loud. One of the blanks has been filled in for you.

Judge _____ entered the court room in his black __gown__
       _{name 1}   _{thing}

and _____ at his bench. He banged his _____ to get
     _{action word}   _{thing}

everyone's attention. The first case involved two people who had

been in a _____ accident. "She ran a _____ light and
         _{thing}   _{color}

_____ed my car," said the man. "That's a _____ lie!"
 _{action word}   _{describing word}

said the woman. "My light was yellow. You _____ed too soon."
                                          _{action word}

They got into a _____ argument. "_____!"
            _{describing word}   _{exclamation}

thundered the judge. "Each of you must pay for your own _____.
                                                  _{things}

Case dismissed!"

CONSTITUTION GARDENS

With a lake, meadows, trees, ducks, and a man-made island, Constitution Gardens is a fine place for picnicking. Then stroll to the **Vietnam Veterans Memorial**. The **Wall**, as it's known, is a large "V" inscribed with the names of the more than 58,000 Americans killed or missing-in-action in the Vietnam War.

In 1950, the United States came to the defense of South Korea after North Korean troops crossed the border between the two countries. At the **Korean War Veterans Memorial**, 19 larger-than-life steel statues of soldiers seem to be walking across the terrain. Why 19 soldiers? Because when they are reflected in the wall behind them, they appear to be 38 in number. The border between North and South Korea is known as the 38th parallel.

A contest was held for the design of the Vietnam Veterans Memorial. The winner, beating out 1,420 others, was a college student named Maya Lin.

⬆ **Thousands of people visit the Wall each year to remember Vietnam War soldiers.**

⬆ **The soldiers of the Korean War Veterans Memorial appear to be marching across the field.**

TWO PRESIDENTS' MEMORIALS

Thomas Jefferson was the nation's first secretary of state, second vice president, and third president. In his spare time, Jefferson invented household devices, played instruments, and designed buildings. The nation's memorial to this remarkable man was built to look like some of his favorite structures: it's not too large, it's round, and it's capped with a small dome. A 19-foot statue of Jefferson stands inside the memorial.

Near the **Jefferson Memorial** stands the newest monument to a great American president on the National Mall: the **Franklin Delano Roosevelt Memorial**. Roosevelt, or FDR, as he is known, was elected president four times, more than any other president. FDR held that office from 1933 until his death in 1945. The FDR Memorial includes four large outdoor rooms spread over seven acres of park land and waterfalls. The site was the first memorial in Washington, D.C., specifically designed to be wheelchair accessible—which is appropriate, because FDR was the first president with a disability that required him to use a wheelchair or leg braces to get around.

⇑ **The Jefferson Memorial glows at night.**

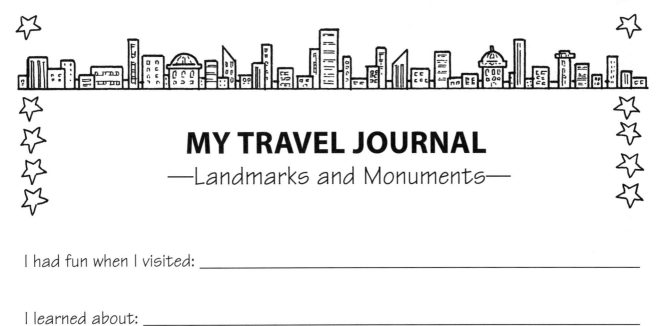

MY TRAVEL JOURNAL
—Landmarks and Monuments—

I had fun when I visited: _____

I learned about: _____

My favorite building was: _____

This is a picture of a building I saw •••

5 GOOD SPORTS

WASHINGTONIANS ARE FAMOUS FOR working too much, but they play a lot, too. Nearly everywhere you go in the city you'll see people running, cycling, stretching, and otherwise exercising their bodies. There's plenty of room for you, too, on the bike paths, hiking trails, fields, and skating rinks. If it's spectator sports you crave, the D.C. area is home to professional teams in basketball, baseball, football, soccer, and hockey. Washington's college teams bring their own brand of excitement to spectator sports, especially basketball. Add to all this the Legg Mason Tennis Classic, the Kemper Open Golf Tournament, and Lincoln Memorial polo—and you've got sports for every season.

⇡ **"Batter up!" A Frederick Keys player gets ready to swing.**

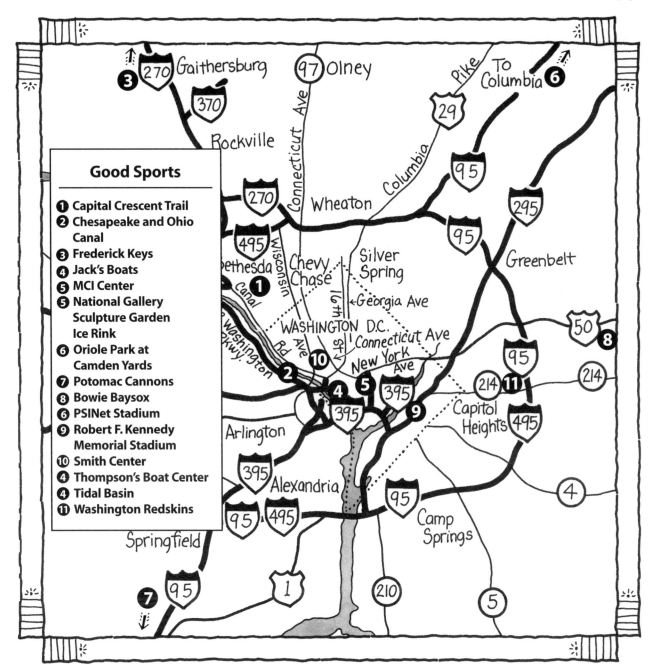

Good Sports

1. **Capital Crescent Trail**
2. **Chesapeake and Ohio Canal**
3. **Frederick Keys**
4. **Jack's Boats**
5. **MCI Center**
5. **National Gallery Sculpture Garden Ice Rink**
6. **Oriole Park at Camden Yards**
7. **Potomac Cannons**
8. **Bowie Baysox**
6. **PSINet Stadium**
9. **Robert F. Kennedy Memorial Stadium**
10. **Smith Center**
4. **Thompson's Boat Center**
4. **Tidal Basin**
11. **Washington Redskins**

SLAM DUNKING

D.C. is jumping from November to April, as the NBA **Washington Wizards** dribble, pass, shoot—and jump!—at their downtown arena, the **MCI Center**. Tickets to Wizards games are not hard to find. While you're at the game, visit the MCI Center's **National Sports Gallery**, where you can play electronic sports games and see cool things from American sports history. The basketball action at the MCI Center continues when the **Washington Mystics**, a Women's National Basketball Association team, take to the floor during the summer months. Mystics forward Chamique Holdsclaw was the WNBA's 1999 rookie of the year.

The capital area is jumping with college basketball teams, too. The Big East **Georgetown Hoyas**, a national championship team, also play at the MCI Center. Enjoy more basketball fun at the **Smith Center** in downtown D.C., where the Atlantic 10 **George Washington Colonials** play.

⬆ Fancy footwork helps a Washington Wizard keep the ball away from the other team.

What's a Hoya? The Georgetown team used to be called the Stonewalls. Students cheered on their team by shouting "Hoya saxa!" which means "What rocks!" in Latin and Greek. So a Hoya is … a "what."

HOYA HOOPLA

Can you help Jack the Bulldog, the Hoyas' mascot, dribble his way to the basket?

AT THE BALL PARK

The last time Major League baseball was played in Washington was in 1971, when the Washington Senators took to the field for their final game. But that doesn't mean the city and its visitors are without baseball. About a million Washingtonians a year travel north to Baltimore to cheer on the three-time world champions, the **Baltimore Orioles**. One of baseball's most famous players is the Orioles' Cal Ripken, who holds the record for the most games played in a row. He broke Lou Gehrig's record of 2,130.

The D.C. area also has three minor league baseball teams and they're major league fun. The **Bowie Baysox** and **Frederick Keys** are both Orioles' farm teams, and the **Potomac Cannons** is a farm team for the St. Louis Cardinals. If you get to the games early, the players are usually happy to talk and sign autographs.

⬆ **A Baysox player signs a baseball for young fans.**

Baseball great Babe Ruth was born in the neighborhood that is now occupied by the Baltimore Orioles' stadium. Beyond the outfield wall you can now visit the Babe Ruth Museum.

TAKE ME OUT TO THE BALL GAME

Hidden in this word search are some things you might see at a baseball game. Search for words vertically, horizontally, and diagonally. Can you find all 12 words? The first word has been found for you.

```
F P I T C H E R S O P M B A S E S
B T C J K D Q S Y M D E M N O N L
N M A S C O T I N L P T S B L T F
S T T O D R S P E A N U T S L U X
U K C F G M N I D U C E N T E D F
M L H N M D F N R N N O G T Y G H
P D E M G T N E H U I U Y E B L J
I O R F U V M N D K F L M R A O F
R P I O U O R O W B C A H F Q V G
E I Z C H S U R N P Y D N L L E B
G N F D L K I T I C K E T S N F S
V C O A C H P Y F R I X B E L Q R
```

FOOTBALL AND SOCCER

Football fans in Washington have to face this fact: their best chance to see their beloved **Redskins** is on television. With only eight home games a season and a gazillion season ticket holders, there are just about no seats for the general public at the team's 80,000-seat stadium in Prince George's County, Maryland.

There are other opportunities to attend football games in the area, however. Since 1998, the **Baltimore Ravens** have been playing at **PSINet Stadium** near Baltimore's Inner Harbor. The Ravens reserve several thousand tickets for each game to sell to the public. And even if you can't snag tickets to an American football game in the nation's capital, you can see soccer, the other "football." Washington is home to a Major League Soccer team, **D.C. United**. The team's matches take place at **Robert F. Kennedy Memorial Stadium** from April to September.

⇡ **The Redskins score a touchdown at their home field.**

⇡ **D.C. United heads the ball in a semifinals game.**

D.C. United holds a slew of top titles in the soccer world. It won the Major League Soccer championships in 1999, 1997, and 1996, and took the 1996 U.S. Open Cup and 1998 Interamerican Cup.

WHAT'S WRONG HERE?

It's a strange day at the stadium and lots of things are out of place.
Name at least 12 things that you think are wrong in this picture.
Circle them when you find them and then color the scene.

SPORTS FOR YOU

The Potomac River is more than just a pretty backdrop to the capital's famous monuments—it's also a fine place to fish and boat. Rent a canoe or kayak from **Thompson's Boat Center** or **Jack's Boats** and explore nearby Roosevelt Island or Georgetown from the water. Or, take a spin on the **Tidal Basin** in a pedal boat, which is like bicycling on water!

If you prefer to do your cycling on land, Washington has plenty of bike paths. The **Capital Crescent Trail** runs from Georgetown to Bethesda, Maryland. No cars allowed! Most bike paths are also suitable for in-line skating. If you like to do your skating on ice, the **National Gallery Sculpture Garden Ice Rink** is the place for you in winter. Where else can you ice skate among famous works of art?

⬆ **Cruising along on the Capital Crescent Trail**

The Washington Capitals, the 1998 National Hockey League Eastern Conference Champions, play ice hockey from October to April at the MCI Center.

MY TRAVEL JOURNAL
—Good Sports—

I had fun when I visited:

_____

I learned about: _____

My favorite sport is: _____

This is a picture of something I saw

6 MUSEUMS AND MORE

FIRST, HERE'S THE SCOOP ON THE Smithsonian: native Washingtonians will know you're in the know if you never ask, "Where's the Smithsonian?" That's because the Smithsonian is in 15 different places in Washington, D.C., counting the National Zoo (which is "the Smithsonian" too!). Most of the Smithsonian's museums are on or near the National Mall, a 146-acre green space where national celebrations are held. They cover exhibits on science, nature, and art, including the only museum in the United States devoted to African art. Whether your interests are diamonds or dinos, you're likely to find what you're looking for at a Smithsonian museum or in the rest of Washington's museums.

⬆ **A spacecraft at the National Air and Space Museum**

Museums

❶ **Bureau of Engraving and Printing**
❷ **Capital Children's Museum**
❸ **Federal Bureau of Investigation (FBI)**
❹ **Hirshhorn Museum**
❺ **Library of Congress**
❻ **National Air and Space Museum**
❼ **National Archives**
❽ **National Gallery of Art**
❾ **National Geographic Society's Explorers Hall**
❿ **National Museum of African Art**
⓫ **National Museum of American History**
⓬ **National Museum of Natural History**
⓭ **National Museum of Women in the Arts**
⓮ **Newseum**
⓯ **Washington Navy Yard and Museum**

NATIONAL AIR AND SPACE MUSEUM

This three-block building on the Mall is said to be the most popular museum in the world, attracting 10 million visitors each year. Be prepared to look up because many exhibits hang from the ceiling. Imagine piloting the tiny *Kitty Hawk Flyer*, used by the Wright brothers for the first manned flight in 1903. Take a look at the toy-like *Apollo 11* Command Module, the vehicle that took the first men to the moon. There's more, including the interactive **How Things Fly** gallery.

And what's a space museum without a planetarium? The **Albert Einstein Planetarium** is one of the most advanced in world. The museum's **Samuel P. Langley Theater** shows films on special IMAX screens that are as tall as a five-story building. Before you leave, be sure to touch a moon rock. It doesn't feel anything like green cheese.

Many of the objects in the Air and Space Museum are truly huge. How did they fit in the door? They didn't. The building's glass walls fold open so large aircraft, missiles, and other exhibits can be moved in and out.

An Eastern Airlines Douglas DC3 on display at the Air and Space Museum

LOST IN SPACE

Without telling anyone what you're doing, ask for a word to fill in each blank. For example, "Give me an action word." When all the blanks are filled in, read the story out loud. One of the blanks has been filled in for you.

_____ and her sister, Shauna, were visiting the Air and Space
girl's name 1

_____. "Look at this neat _____," said Shauna. "Let's
place thing

sit inside." The two girls _____ed it. Suddenly the shuttle
action word

began to ____**rattle**____ and shake. Before the girls knew what to do,
sound

it had _____ed them into space! "_____!" squealed
action word exclamation

Shauna. "We're at least _____ miles from_____. How
number place

will we get back?" Her sister reached up and pushed the blue

_____. Instantly they were back at the museum.
thing

NATIONAL MUSEUM OF NATURAL HISTORY

You know you're in the right place when you're greeted inside the front door by an African elephant as tall as a small apartment building. This is the museum of animals, gemstones, mummies, and more. If dinosaur bones are your thing, go to **Dinosaur Hall.** Way back in 1923, it took scientists half a year to pry the the 72-foot-long *Diplodocus* skeleton out of the ground.

Then it took seven years to put it back together. This museum has a terrific collection of touchable goodies, too. Follow your fingers to the first-floor **Discovery Room,** where you can handle animal skulls, tusks, minerals, beetles, petrified wood, and other items from the world of nature. Creepy crawly things like spiders, ants, and tarantulas have a home in the **Orkin Insect Zoo** on the second floor.

The National Museum of the American Indian opens on the Mall in 2002 with thousands of objects covering 10,000 years of history.

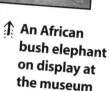

⬆ **An African bush elephant on display at the museum**

WHAT'S MISSING HERE?

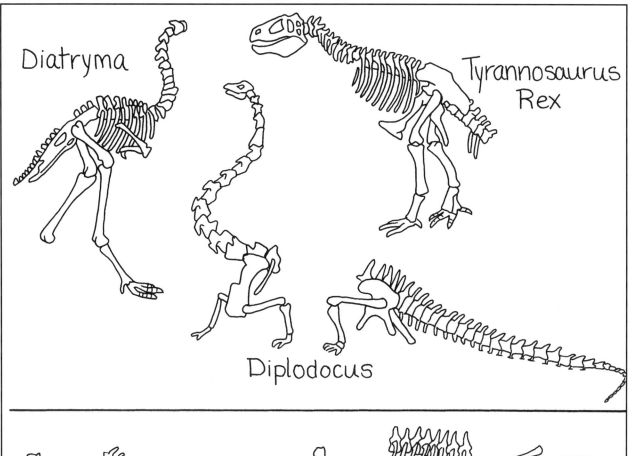

Diatryma

Tyrannosaurus
Rex

Diplodocus

**These dinosaurs are each missing two pieces of their skeletons. Draw
lines from the missing pieces to the dinosaur they belong to.**

NATIONAL MUSEUM OF AMERICAN HISTORY

When you've seen the collection of stuff in the American history museum, you'll know why the Smithsonian is called the "nation's attic." You'll find the original Mr. Potato Head toy in one gallery, the original "Star-Spangled Banner" in another, and even the ruby slippers that Dorothy wore in *The Wizard of Oz*, as well as the formal gowns worn by the nation's first ladies. Spend some time among computers, telephones, and technology in **Information Age: People, Information and Technology**, one of the largest exhibits ever. Other popular exhibits are **Money and Metals** and the automobile collection in **Road Transportation**.

The museum has two mini-museums especially for children. Pedal an old-fashioned high-wheeler bicycle in the **Hands on History Room**. In the **Hands on Science Center**, you can conduct laboratory tests and see for yourself how science shapes our lives.

⇒

Dorothy's famous ruby slippers are on display at the National Museum of American History.

A SPECIAL DISPLAY

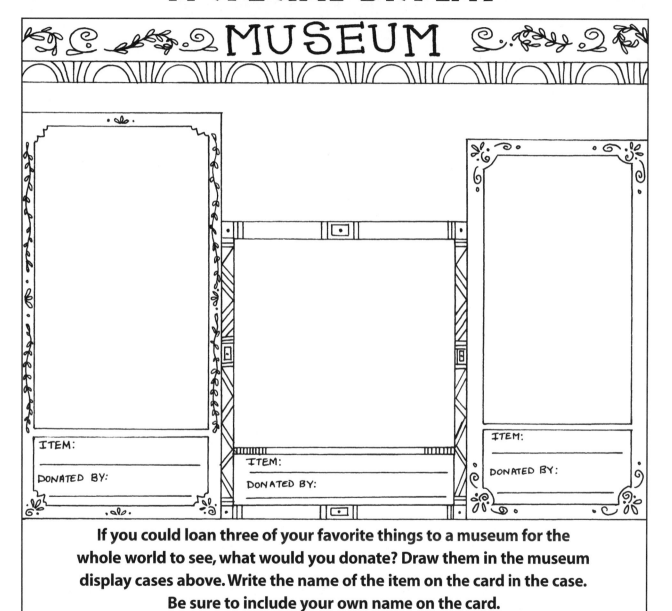

MUSEUM

ITEM:

DONATED BY:

ITEM:

DONATED BY:

ITEM:

DONATED BY:

If you could loan three of your favorite things to a museum for the whole world to see, what would you donate? Draw them in the museum display cases above. Write the name of the item on the card in the case. Be sure to include your own name on the card.

BUREAU OF ENGRAVING AND PRINTING/FBI

↥ **Money being printed**

The outside of the **Bureau of Engraving and Printing** looks kind of run-down, but don't be fooled. They have plenty of money here. This is where all the nation's paper money is made, along with postage stamps, savings bonds, and White House invitations. On the tour, you'll see stacks of sheets of newly printed money. Government workers examine the money for defects. They don't give away free samples, but defective money is shredded and sold by the bag at the gift shop.

If you take a tour of the **Federal Bureau of Investigation**, you'll see loot and thousands of guns that have been recovered from criminals. In the crime labs, you may see scientists working with fingerprints and microscopes to solve an actual case. The tour ends with a bang as FBI agents demonstrate target shooting at an indoor shooting range.

Our currency is made of cotton and linen. The average dollar bill falls apart after 18 months, and can be folded 8,000 times before it tears. Made of plain paper, a dollar would last only a week.

WHAT'S THE DIFFERENCE?

One of the dollar bills below is different than the others. Use your detective skills to help determine which bill is flawed.

WASHINGTON NAVY YARD AND MUSEUM

The Navy Yard was once the largest shipbuilding center in the United States. Today its old gun factory houses an exciting museum with lots to keep you busy. A U.S. Navy destroyer, the USS *Barry*, is docked in front of the museum and is open to the public. As you squeeze through the narrow doorways, try to imagine sharing this ship with 350 other people. Sailors can't be picky about privacy! Inside the spacious museum, you can climb on the bridge of the USS *Fletcher*, man the large gunmount of the battleship USS *South Dakota*, and command the fighting top of the USF *Constitution*. By the time you operate the periscope and steering wheels in the **Submarine Museum**, you'll be an old sea hand.

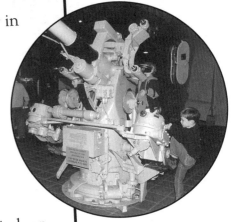

⇧ **Hands-on fun at the Navy Museum**

⇐ **Pools of water taken from each of the world's seven seas surround the granite map at the U.S. Navy Memorial.**

For more seafaring stuff, and a chance to walk all over the largest map of the world in the world, go to the U.S. Navy Memorial. It also shows the IMAX film *At Sea*.

TREASURE HUNT

**Debbie the diver has been searching for a sunken treasure chest.
Can you help her swim through the maze and strike it rich?**

ART GALLERIES

Even the buildings are beautiful at the **National Gallery of Art** on the Mall. Inside the West Building you'll find paintings by famous artists such as Rembrandt, Van Gogh, Renoir, and da Vinci. The East Building displays mostly modern art. Across the Mall is the doughnut-shaped **Hirshhorn Museum**. Many well-known modern artists' pictures are here, including one by Pablo Picasso. On a nice day, visit the Hirshhorn's outdoor **Sculpture Garden**. Check out *Man Pushing the Door* and you'll see how exciting sculpture can be.

⬆ **The round Hirshhorn Museum at night**

The **National Museum of African Art** shows that art is not limited to pictures and sculptures. Examine objects such as wooden stools, hair ornaments, and headrests, and you'll see how art is woven into everyday life in Africa. And although most of the artwork displayed in the nation's galleries is by famous men, this is not so at the **National Museum of Women in the Arts**—a refreshing change, whether you're a boy or a girl.

CROSSWORD FUN

There are lots of things to see at Washington's art galleries. Solve this crossword by figuring out the clues or completing the sentences. If you need help, use the clue box.

Across

1. You put this around a painting. Some are quite fancy.
5. The National Galley of Art building with mostly modern art.
7. You might give a piece of art as a _____ to someone.
8. *Man Pushing the Door* is an example of this.

Down

2. Painters, sculptors, and cartoonists are all _____.
3. When it comes to art, beauty is in the _____ of the beholder.
4. The shape of the Hirshhorn Museum, or a breakfast treat.
6. A building that houses art is sometimes called this.

Clue Box

gallery	eye
sculpture	frame
artists	east
doughnut	gift

LIBRARY OF CONGRESS AND NATIONAL ARCHIVES

You can't borrow any books during your tour of the Library of Congress, but you can get a look at the impressive **Main Reading Room** of the world's largest library. You'll also see a Gutenberg Bible dating from 1455. It was one of the first books ever printed by movable metal type. The Library of Congress started in 1800 as a reference library for members of Congress. Today the library has more than 116 million books, newspapers, maps, and other items, and it grows 10,000 items bigger every day!

Another place with plenty on hand to read is the **National Archives**. This is where America's history is kept safe. The original Declaration of Independence, Constitution, and Bill of Rights are displayed in special glass and bronze cases. Every night the documents are lowered into a vault underneath the floor.

⬆ The library's Main Reading Room

The smallest book in the Library of Congress is *Old King Cole*. It is roughly the size of the period at the end of this sentence. The pages can be turned with a needle.

⬆ The Declaration of Independence on display at the National Archives

WHERE DO THEY BELONG?

A shelf of library books has fallen. Can you help Larry the librarian put them back on the shelf in alphabetical order? Draw a line from the book to the correct place on the shelf. The first one has been done for you.

HANDS-ON FUN

Get ready to stop sight*seeing* and start sight*doing* at the **Capital Children's Museum.** Grind your own chocolate and corn for a snack of hot chocolate and tortillas in the **Mexico Exhibit.** Then move on to **Japan: The Land of the Rising Sun,** which features a simulated ride on Japan's famous "bullet" train. At the **National Geographic Society's Explorers Hall,** interactive stations let you experience other lands, bodies of water, and weather systems. Check out the giant globe and watch the two movies.

The **Newseum,** in nearby Arlington, Virginia, is all about journalism. Join the staff of the Newseum's newspaper, the *Daily Miracle,* and make decisions about how to cover events in the fictional town of Medina. See what it's like to be a television journalist reading the day's news in front of the cameras. Play one of the journalism games on the 32 interactive game stations. Have a snack at the **News Byte Café,** and use one of the Internet stations there to surf more than 1,000 on-line news sites.

Experience a Mexican marketplace at the Children's Museum.

Practice your television journalism skills at the Newseum.

MY TRAVEL JOURNAL
—Museums and More—

I had fun when I visited: _____

My favorite museum was: _____

What I enjoyed doing there the most was: _____

This is a picture of something I saw • • •

7 THAT'S ENTERTAINMENT

SIGHTSEEING IS FUN, BUT EVERYONE needs a change of pace sometimes. When you're ready for a break from museums and monuments, Washington offers plenty of ways to kick back and have fun. From mega-malls to military music, there's entertainment everywhere. To find out what special events are planned when you're in town, call the Washington, D.C. Convention and Visitors Association. The free *City Paper*, the Friday Weekend section of the *Washington Post*, and the monthly *Washingtonian* magazine are all good places to look for information about what's happening. And don't forget to check out the Calendar section at the back of this book.

⬆ **A puppet performs at the Puppet Co. in Glen Echo Park.**

That's Entertainment

1. **Chevy Chase Pavilion**
2. **Discovery Theater**
3. **Fashion Centre at Pentagon City**
4. **Georgetown Park**
1. **Glen Echo Park**
1. **Jeepers**
5. **Kennedy Center**
1. **Mazza Gallerie**
6. **National Theater**
3. **Potomac Mills**
7. **Shops at National Place**
8. **Six Flags America**
9. **Union Station**

WASHINGTON'S OTHER MALLS

The museum-filled National Mall isn't the only kind of mall in D.C. There are plenty of other malls—for shopping, not sightseeing. Start your shopping spree at **Georgetown Park**, a fancy mall in the heart of old Georgetown that has an **FAO Schwarz** toy store, a shop for animal lovers called **The Magical Animal**, and about 100 other stores. Then visit the **Shops at National Place**, three levels of shops and eateries in the heart of downtown. Next, move uptown. On top of the Friendship Heights Metro stop, the light-filled **Chevy Chase Pavilion** has 50 shops. Across the street is **Mazza Gallerie**.

You say you want more? Visit the 160-store **Fashion Centre at Pentagon City**, which also sits atop a Metro stop. If you think bigger is better, head 30 minutes south of D.C. to **Potomac Mills**. With 1.7 million square feet of space, 52 acres of parking, and more than 200 stores, it's the ultimate discount mall.

⇧ **The Chevy Chase Pavilion**

You can board a train at Union Station and head out of town, but why not stay and visit the shops and restaurants? Don't miss the working railroad models at the Great Train Store.

TRACE THE TRACKS

These trains just left their stations. By tracing their tracks, can you tell which station each train started from? Draw lines from the trains to the correct stations.

SIX FLAGS AMERICA

If it's excitement you're after, an amusement park is the place to go. Six Flags America is the closest. It's got more than 100 rides, shows, and attractions, featuring some of your favorite animated characters, from Bugs Bunny to Daffy Duck. For thrill-seekers, there's **The Joker's Jinx**, a super-powered ride that blasts you from 0 to 60 miles per hour in three seconds. **Two-Face the Flip Side** roller coaster sends you backwards, forwards—and straight up. After the scary thrills, the **Looney Tunes Show**, a family-style musical, might be the perfect way to relax. Then head over to **Paradise Island**, Six Flags' water park. Splash around in a five-story water treehouse, ride the water slides, float down **Castaway Creek** in a tube, or swim in **Monsoon Lagoon**, one of the largest wave pools in the United States.

Not up for theme park thrills? **Jeepers** has indoor roller coasters, bumper cars, skill games, and other indoor amusement park rides.

⇧ **Thrill-seekers hurtle over the Superman roller coaster.**

WHAT'S WRONG HERE?

It's a strange day at the amusement park and lots of things are out of place. Name at least 12 things that you think are wrong in this picture. Circle them when you find them and then color the scene.

OUTDOOR CONCERTS

After you've put in a full day of seeing the city, and if you're visiting between May and September, you can top off your day with a very Washingtonian form of entertainment: an evening of free music under the stars. Just about every night, the **U.S. Marine Band, Navy Band,** or **Army Band** performs on the National Mall. For a unique experience, attend a **Twilight Tattoo** on the Ellipse behind the White House. There, the U.S. Army Drill Team and Army Band, along with their Fife and Drum Corps, show off their fancy footwork and play music at the same time.

You can listen to concert tunes with the tigers at the **National Zoo Sunset Serenades**. Lie on a blanket on Lion-Tiger Hill, close your eyes, and enjoy the night sounds.

⬆ **The Army Band in parade**

What's a military tattoo? No, it's not a picture on a sailor's muscle. It's an evening exercise, usually with drums and bugles, and was originally used to tell soldiers it was bedtime.

TUNE TIME

Hidden in this word search are some things you might see at a musical concert. Search for words vertically, horizontally, and diagonally. Can you find all 10 words? The first word has been found for you.

Clue Box		
microphone	baton	conductor
stage	drum	musician
trumpet	violin	bow
music stand		

```
B D L V T S T A G E P M Y P V U A
M J T R U M P E T M H E B A O N S
I Z H X S O M U S I C S T A N D D
C J F Z B R S K B X I N G U L N M
R K T A G A N R D V C E N T I V U
O U U Q M D T N G N N O G L Y E S
P D I W G U N O H U I U O E B W I
H S D R U M I K N K C I M R A D C
O L P R J K R O W B V A T F L Q I
N H L T I W U R N P Y D N L L U A
E V M C O N D U C T O R M Y N F N
A W S B I O P Y F R I C L E E Q R
```

KENNEDY CENTER

⬆ **Flags from all 50 states in the Hall of States**

This huge performing arts center has six theaters that present drama, dance, music, movies, and more. It's an exciting place to attend a performance, and there are many programs just for kids. Inside, you can't miss the huge **Hall of Nations** where the flags of more than 165 countries hang in alphabetical order, from Albania to Zimbabwe. On the other side is the **Hall of States**, where the flags of the 50 states are hung in the order in which they joined the United States. How many flags do you recognize? You can get a sheet that identifies each nation and state flag at the Information Center.

You'll also want to see the massive bronze sculpture of President John F. Kennedy in the **Grand Foyer**. It's 7 feet high and weighs 3,000 pounds.

The Kennedy Center's Grand Foyer is one of the largest rooms in the world. The Washington Monument would easily fit on its side in the 630-foot foyer.

⬅ **The John F. Kennedy Center**

WHAT'S IN COMMON?

Each of these flags has something in common with the other two in the same row. For example, all of the flags in the top row have a triangle on them. Draw a line through each row and describe what the flags in that row have in common. Don't forget to include diagonals!

CHILDREN'S THEATER

Mimes, magicians, musicians, and more—let them entertain you at one of Washington's special theaters for kids. **Discovery Theater**, located in the Smithsonian's Arts and Industries Building on the National Mall, stages all kinds of shows throughout the week.

The downtown **National Theater** is one of the oldest playhouses in the country, but they know what today's kids like. See for yourself at the Saturday morning programs held throughout the school year. A short drive away in Maryland, **Glen Echo Park** is home to **Adventure Theater** and the **Puppet Co**. Glen Echo used to be an amusement park, and Adventure Theater puts on plays for children in the park's old penny arcade. The Puppet Co. takes to the stage in the Spanish Ballroom, using marionettes, hand puppets, rod puppets, and shadows. Sit down on the carpeted floor and let the puppets perform!

⇡ **The bright and beautiful Dentzel carousel at Glen Echo**

At Glen Echo, you can ride a beautiful old Dentzel carousel, originally made in 1921. The carousel has 1,200 lights, 52 hand-carved wood figures, and a Wurlitzer organ.

MY TRAVEL JOURNAL
—That's Entertainment—

These are the names of the places I visited: _____

My favorite place was: _____

What I enjoyed doing the most was: _____

This is a picture of something I saw

8 LET'S EAT!

SOME CITIES ARE KNOWN FOR A particular type of food. There's Chicago pizza, New York bagels, and New Orleans gumbo. The nation's capital is a different story. There's no single food that has Washington's stamp on it. Instead, there are many types of food, probably because people from all over the country (and the world) come here to live. You can enjoy down-home Southern cooking, crab feasts, elegant European food, or a great hamburger. If you're adventurous, you'll want to sample ethnic foods from Asia, the Caribbean, Africa, the Middle East, and almost any other region you might care to name. So, tuck your napkin under your chin and dig in!

Check out movie souvenirs while you eat at Planet Hollywood.

Let's Eat

1. A.V.
2. Capitol eateries
3. Cascade Cafe
4. Clyde's
5. Clyde's (Chevy Chase)
6. Dancing Crab
7. Georgia Brown's
8. Hard Rock Café
9. Houston's
10. Marrakesh
11. Music City Roadhouse
12. National Air and Space Museum eateries
13. National Museum of American History eateries
14. Planet Hollywood
15. Red Sea
16. Reeves Restaurant & Bakery
17. Sholl's Colonial Cafeteria
18. Sherrill's Bakery
19. Supreme Court Cafeteria
20. Zed's Ethiopian Cuisine

FINGER FOODS

In many cultures, eating with your hands is the accepted way to enjoy a fine meal. At **Marrakesh**, you can order a seven-course Moroccan feast—and there's not a knife or fork in sight. You eat it all with your fingers as you sit on comfy sofas and listen to Moroccan music. At **Zed's Ethiopian Cuisine**, and the **Red Sea**, you eat the spicy food by scooping it up with special bread called *injera*.

If you're handy with a hammer, you'll be good at getting the meat out of steamed blue crabs, a specialty from the nearby Chesapeake Bay. At the **Dancing Crab** the "silverware" is wooden hammers called mallets. Finally, although some people eat pizza with a knife and fork, it's not necessary at the **A.V.**, where people have been picking up the crispy white pizza for more than 50 years.

If you order blue crabs and they come to the table bright red, that's okay. The crabs change color when when they're cooked.

⇐ **Using bread to scoop up Ethiopian food at Zed's**

COLOR TO FIND THE ANSWER

What animal crawls sideways, changes color when it's cooked, and is eaten with a fork and a hammer? Color the shapes with numbers in them blue. Color the other shapes any colors you want.

BEST BURGER BETS

Yes, D.C. has McDonald's, Wendy's, and Burger King, but you can do better than that to satisfy your hunger for a hamburger. Washingtonians argue about where to get the best burger in town, but many agree that one of the best is at **Houston's**. If you're willing to join the crowds, you can combine hamburgers with entertainment and music at **Planet Hollywood** and the **Hard Rock Café,** both a few blocks from the National Mall.

Finally, **Clyde's** has been a hot hamburger (and chili) spot in Georgetown for more than 30 years. But the newer **Clyde's** in Chevy Chase, Maryland, is the place to see. It's filled with racing cars and fabulous model airplanes and ships. While you eat, a model train races around overhead.

⇡ **Palm trees in Washington? Only at Planet Hollywood!**

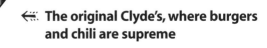

⇐ **The original Clyde's, where burgers and chili are supreme**

MATCH THE BURGERS

Find the hamburger on the left that matches the one on the right.
Connect the matching hamburgers with a line.

HOMETOWN TASTE

You may be in the big city, but you can get cozy home-style cooking in Washington. If soup and a sandwich with layer cake for dessert is your perfect lunch, **Reeves Restaurant & Bakery** and **Sherrill's Bakery** are for you. They both bake their own pastries. Both serve breakfast, too. If you like lots of choices, get in line at **Sholl's Colonial Cafeteria** for breakfast, lunch, or dinner.

⬆ **Snacking at Sholl's Colonial Cafeteria**

Try home-style Southern cooking at the **Music City Roadhouse** where they serve up giant portions of Southern favorites. You'll be treated to live gospel music if you come for Sunday brunch. For a quieter, more elegant meal, let your parents take you to **Georgia Brown's**. It's pretty fancy Southern cooking, but not so fancy that you can't dig into the bread basket for seconds of the cornbread.

Reeves Restaurant & Bakery has been around since 1886. They still make sandwiches the old-fashioned way—on home-baked bread with homemade mayonnaise.

HIDE AND SEEK!

Can you find the hidden objects in this picture? When you find one,
draw a circle around it. When you're done, color the scene.
Look for: bell, hand, butterfly, boot, penguin, pencil, chicken leg, sucker,
banana, ladybug, ice cream cone, baseball bat, heart, candle.

SIGHTSEEING SNACKS

Where can you eat when you're in the middle of a busy day of sightseeing? Right in the middle of the sights, of course. Many museums have restaurants and cafés, and two of the best are in the National Air and Space Museum. The **Flight Line Cafeteria** offers everything from soup to hot main courses to fresh-baked desserts. **Wright Place** is a café with a children's menu. The National Gallery of Art's **Cascade Café** is another good spot on the Mall. The National Museum of American History has two kid-friendly choices: a big, bustling cafeteria and **Palm Court**, an ice cream parlor.

Places to eat on Capitol Hill include the buffet in the Dirksen Senate Office Building and the cafeteria in the Library of Congress's James Madison Building. Or have an inexpensive legal lunch at the **Supreme Court Cafeteria**. Keep your eyes open for the Supreme Court justices who sometimes eat there.

Bean soup has been served every day in the Senate restaurants for nearly 100 years, but no one really knows why.

Dining at Wright Place in the National Air and Space Museum

MY TRAVEL JOURNAL
—Let's Eat!—

These are the names of some of the restaurants I ate at:

_____

My favorite restaurant was: _____

The food I enjoyed there the most was: _____

This is a picture of one restaurant I visited

CALENDAR OF WASHINGTON, D.C., EVENTS

January

Martin Luther King Jr. Day

Various locations, (202) 619-7222 or (202) 426-6841. The birthday of the slain civil rights leader is observed on the third Monday of the month with special events and performances.

February

Chinese New Year Celebration

Chinatown, (202) 357-2700. Colorful floats, dancers, dragons, parades, and fireworks mark the lunar year celebration. Look, listen, and lunch!

March

White House Easter Egg Roll

White House lawn, (202) 456-2200.
A limited number of tickets are available at the White House Visitor Center.

St. Patrick's Day Parade

Constitution Avenue, (202) 789-7000.

Smithsonian Kite Festival

Washington Monument grounds, (202) 357-2700.

April

National Cherry Blossom Festival

Tidal Basin, (202) 619-7222 or 789-7000. This springtime tradition celebrates the 3,300 flowering cherry trees (a gift of the Japanese government) planted around the Tidal Basin. There's a lantern lighting, a parade, fireworks, and hopefully, the March winds or April showers haven't blown the blossoms away.

White House Spring Garden Tours

(202) 456-2200.

Imagination Celebration

John F. Kennedy Center for the Performing Arts, (202) 416-8340. For the entire month, children's theater companies from around the country perform.

May

Washington National Cathedral Flower Mart

(202) 537-6200. They sell spring flowers at this two-day event, but that's not all. There are fun carnival rides for kids, food, performances, and a cake walk.

Andrews Air Force Base Air Show

Camp Springs, Maryland, (301) 981-1110.

Memorial Day Concert

U.S. Capitol, (202) 426-6841, (202) 619-7222. The National Symphony Orchestra gives a free concert at the West Lawn of the U.S. Capitol.

June

Shakespeare Free for All
Carter Barron Amphitheater, (202) 547-3230.

Festival of American Folklife
National Mall, (202) 357-2700. Since 1966, this ten-day event features exhibits, food, and performances celebrating America's heritage.

Juneteenth
The Anacostia Museum, (202) 287-2061. Celebrate June 19, the day when Texas slaves learned they were free—two years after President Lincoln issued the Emancipation Proclamation.

Alexandria Red Cross Waterfront Festival
Potomac River waterfront, (202) 426-6841, (703) 549-8300. An impressive display of tall ships along with games, entertainment, and food.

July

National Independence Day Celebration
Various locations, (202) 426-6841, (202) 619-7222. See a parade down Constitution Avenue, free entertainment during the day at the Sylvan Theater, a nighttime National Symphony Orchestra concert on the Mall, and spectacular fireworks show.

U.S. Army Band 1812 Overture Concert
Sylvan Theater, (202) 619-7222 or (202) 426-6841.

Waterlily Festival
Kenilworth Gardens, (202) 426-6905.

August

Legg Mason Tennis Classic
William H.G. Fitzgerald Tennis Center, (202) 432-SEAT.

Montgomery County Agricultural Fair
Gaithersburg, Maryland, (301) 926-3100.

Navy Band Lollipop Concert
Sylvan Theater, (202) 433-2525 or (202) 619-7222.

Prince William County Fair
Manassas, Virginia, (703) 368-0173.

September

Hispanic Heritage Month
Various locations, (202) 357-4320.

Prince George's County Fair
Upper Marlboro, Maryland, (301) 579-2598.

Maryland State Fair
Timonium, Maryland, (410) 252-0200.

Labor Day Weekend Concert
U.S. Capitol, (202) 426-6841 or (202) 619-7222. The National Symphony's last summer concert, at the West Lawn of the U.S. Capitol.

International Children's Festival
Wolf Trap Farm Park for the Performing Arts, in Vienna, Virginia, (703) 642-0862. Held in early September.

National Frisbee Festival
National Mall, (202) 619-7222 or (202) 426-6841.

Kennedy Center Open House Arts Festival
Kennedy Center, (202) 467-4600. Local performers and artists and lots of audience participation are highlights.

Goddard Space Flight Center Community Day
Goddard Space Flight Center, Greenbelt, Maryland, (301) 286-8981.

October

White House Fall Garden Tours
White House, (202) 456-2200.

Taste of D.C.
Pennsylvania Avenue, (202) 724-5430 or (202) 789-7000. The city's restaurants show off their best cooking.

Theodore Roosevelt's Birthday Celebration
Theodore Roosevelt Island, (703) 289-2550. Take an island tour, learn about wildlife, and enjoy entertainment for kids.

Marine Corps Marathon
Marine Corps Memorial, Arlington, Virginia, (202) 619-7222.

November

Seafaring Celebration
Navy Museum, held the first Saturday in November, (202) 433-4882. Kids can make model ships, periscopes, and kites.

⇡ **The National Christmas Tree Lighting at the Capitol**

Veterans Day Ceremonies
Various locations, (202) 619-7222.

December

Smithsonian Kwanzaa Celebration
Various locations, (202) 357-2700.

The Holidays at Mount Vernon
Mount Vernon, (703) 780-2000.

National Christmas Tree Lighting/Pageant of Peace
White House, (202) 456-2200. Enjoy caroling and a Nativity scene on the Ellipse behind the White House.

White House Christmas Candlelight Tours
(202) 456-2200.

Kennedy Center Holiday Celebrations
John F. Kennedy Center for the Performing Arts, (202) 467-4600.

RESOURCE GUIDE:
WHEN, WHAT, AND HOW MUCH?

Hours and days of operation, as well as prices, are subject to change, so be sure to call the site before you visit. Some attractions close or have special hours on federal holidays.

All the places in this Resource Guide have activities for kids and families. But not every place is suitable; have your parents check before you go.

If You Get Lost

It's a good idea to make a plan with your parents about what to do if you lose them. If you're visiting one of Washington's museums or memorials, go to a uniformed guard, a park ranger, or a police officer. If you're in a store or restaurant, go to the person working behind the cash register. If you're outside, find a mother with children and tell her you're lost.

If you need the police, fire department, or an ambulance, dial 911. You won't need any coins, even at a pay phone.

Important Phone Numbers and Addresses

Injury, accident, or emergency 911
Police (202) 727-1010
Poison Control (202) 625-3333

Tourist Information

Dial-A-Museum, for recorded Smithsonian
  Institution information; (202) 357-2020. In
  Spanish, (202) 633-9126. www.si.edu

Dial-A-Park, for recorded National Park Service
  information; (202) 619-PARK. www.nps.gov
TicketMaster, (800) 551-SEAT or (202) 432-SEAT.
  www.ticketmaster.com
Concert Information:
  U.S. Army Band, (703) 696-3399
  U.S. Marine Band, (202) 433-4011
  U.S. Navy Band, (202) 433-2525

Washington, D.C. Convention and Visitors
  Association, 1212 New York Avenue, N.W., Suite
  600, Washington, D.C. 20005; (202) 789-7000.
  www.washington.org

Public Transportation

Metrorail and Metrobus free guide (202) 635-6434;
schedule information (202) 637-7000.

Attractions

Albert Einstein Planetarium, National Air and Space Museum, Independence Avenue and Seventh Street, S.W. Metro stop: L'Enfant Plaza. Admission $3.75. (202) 357-1686. www.nasm.edu/nasm/planetarium

Arts and Industries Building,
900 Jefferson Drive, S.W., Metro stop: Smithsonian. Open daily from 10 a.m. to 5:30 p.m. Admission free. (202) 357-2700

A.V., 607 New York Avenue, N.W. Metro stop: Gallery Place/Chinatown. Open Monday through Thursday from 11 a.m. to 11 p.m., Friday from 11 a.m. to 12 midnight, Saturday from 5 p.m. to 12 midnight. (202) 737-0550

Babe Ruth Museum, 216 Emory Street, Baltimore, Maryland. Open daily from 10 a.m. to 5 p.m. April to October; 4 p.m. otherwise; open until 7 p.m. when Orioles play at home. Admission $6 for adults, $3 for children ages 5 to 16. Children under 5 are free. (410) 727-1539. www.baberuthmuseum.com

Baltimore Ravens, Ticket Office, 200 St. Paul Place, Suite 2400, Baltimore, Maryland. Call for ticket prices. (410) 261-RAVE. www.baltimoreravens.com

Bowie Baysox, Prince George's Stadium, at Routes 50 and 301, Bowie, Maryland. Admission $4 to $12, children wearing athletic uniforms free. (301) 805-6000. www.baysox.com

Bureau of Engraving and Printing, 14th and C Streets, S.W. Metro stop: Smithsonian. Tours Monday through Friday from 9 a.m. to 2 p.m., also open 5 p.m. to 6:40 p.m. in summer. Ticket booth on Raoul Wallenberg Place; tickets required in summer. Admission free. (202) 874-3188. www.bep.treas.gov

Capital Children's Museum, 800 Third Street, N.E. Metro stop: Union Station. Open Tuesday through Sunday (and holiday Mondays) from 10 a.m. to 5 p.m. Admission $6, free for children under 2. (202) 675-4120. www.ccm.org

Capital Crescent Trail, enter at Key Bridge in Georgetown, or at Woodmont and Bethesda Avenues, Bethesda, Maryland. Admission free. (202) 234-4874. www.cctrail.org

Chesapeake and Ohio Canal National Historical Park, 1057 Thomas Jefferson Street, N.W. Visitor Center at 30th and Thomas Jefferson Streets. Open daily during daylight hours. Admission free. (202) 653-5190. Also at National Park Service, Great Falls Tavern, 11710 MacArthur Boulevard, Potomac, Maryland. Admission $2 per person or $4 per car. (301) 299-2026. (301) 299-3613. www.nps.gov/choh

Chevy Chase Pavilion, 5335 Wisconsin Avenue, N.W. Metro stop: Friendship Heights. Open daily. (202) 686-5335

Claude Moore Colonial Farm, 6310 Georgetown Pike, McLean, Virginia. Open April through mid-December, Wednesday through Sunday from 10 a.m. to 4:30 p.m. Admission $2 for adults, $1 for 14 and under. (703) 442-7557

Clyde's of Georgetown, 3236 M Street, N.W. Open Monday through Friday from 11:30 a.m. to 2 a.m., Saturday and Sunday from 9:30 a.m. to 2 a.m. (202) 333-9180. www.clydes.com

Clyde's of Chevy Chase, 35 Wisconsin Avenue, Chevy Chase, Maryland. Metro stop: Friendship Heights. Open Monday through Saturday from 11 a.m. to 11 p.m., Sunday from 10 a.m. to 11 p.m. (301) 951-9600. www.clydes.com

Constitution Gardens, between 17th and 23rd Streets, N.W. and Constitution Avenue, N.W. Metro stop: Foggy Bottom/George Washington University. (202) 485-9880

Dancing Crab, 4611 Wisconsin Avenue, N.W. Metro stop: Tenleytown/American University. Open Monday through Friday from 11 a.m. to 11 p.m., Saturday from 12 noon to 11 p.m., Sunday from 3 p.m. to 11 p.m. (202) 244-1882

D.C. United, 13832 Redskin Drive, Herndon, Virginia. Tickets $13 to $34. (703) 478-6600. www.dcunited.com

Dirksen South Buffet, Dirksen Senate Office Building, basement, south side. Metro stop: Union Station or Capitol South. Open Monday through Friday from 11:30 a.m. to 2:30 p.m. (202) 224-4249

Discovery Theater, Smithsonian Arts and Industries Building, 900 Jefferson Drive, S.W. Metro stop: Smithsonian. Call for show times and prices. (202) 357-1500. www.si.edu/tsa/disctheater

Emancipation Statue, Lincoln Park, at East Capitol Street between 11th and 13th Streets, N.W. Metro stop: Eastern Market.

Fashion Centre at Pentagon City, 1100 South Hayes Street, Arlington, Virginia. Metro Stop: Pentagon City. Open Monday through Saturday from 10 a.m. to 9:30 p.m., Sunday from 11 a.m. to 6 p.m. (703) 415-2400

Federal Bureau of Investigation, J. Edgar Hoover Building, Pennsylvania Avenue between Ninth and Tenth Streets, N.W. Metro stop: Metro Center. Open Monday through Friday from 8:45 a.m. to 4:15 p.m. Admission free. (202) 324-3447. www.fbi.gov

Fletcher's Boat House, 4940 Canal Road, N.W. Call for hours and prices. (202) 244-0461

Flight Line Cafeteria, National Air and Space Museum, Independence Avenue and Seventh Street, S.W. Metro stop: L'Enfant Plaza. Open daily from 11 a.m. to 5 p.m. (202) 371-8777

Ford's Theater and Lincoln Museum, 511 Tenth Street, N.W. Metro stop: Metro Center. Open daily from 9 a.m. to 5 p.m. except when closed early for performances. Admission free to museum. Museum (202) 426-6924, Theater (202) 347-4833. www.nps.gov/foth

Fort Stevens Park, 13th Street and Piney Branch Road, N.W. Open daily until dusk.

Fort Washington Park, 13551 Fort Washington Road, Fort Washington, Maryland. Open daily, October through March from 9 a.m. to 4:30 p.m., 9 a.m. to 5 p.m. otherwise. Call for tour schedule. Admission free. Parking $4. (301) 763-4600. www.nps.gov/fowa

Franklin Delano Roosevelt Memorial, Tidal Basin at Ohio Drive, S.W. Metro stop: Smithsonian or L'Enfant Plaza. Open daily 8 a.m. to 11:45 p.m. Admission free. (202) 426-6841 or (202) 619-7222. www.nps.gov/fdrm

Frederick Keys, Harry Grove Stadium, Market Street off I-270, Frederick, Maryland. Admission $3 to $9. (301) 831-4200

Freedom Plaza, Pennsylvania Avenue between 13th and 14th Streets, N.W. Metro stop: Federal Triangle.

Georgetown Hoyas, Georgetown University Athletic Ticket Office, McDonough Arena. N.W. Tickets $5 to $35. (202) 687-2449 or (202) 432-SEAT. www.guhoyas.com

Georgetown Park, 3222 M Street, N.W. Shopping mall open daily. (202) 298-5577

George Washington University Colonials, Charles Smith Center, 22nd and G Streets, N.W. Admission $12 to $15, $5 to $7.50 for children. (202) 994-6650

Georgia Brown's, 950 15th Street, N.W. Metro Stop: McPherson Square. Open Monday through Thursday from 11:30 a.m. to 11 p.m., Friday from 11:30 a.m. to midnight, Saturday from 5:30 p.m. to midnight, Sunday from 11:30 a.m. to 3 p.m. and 5:30 p.m. to 11 p.m. (202) 393-4499

Glen Echo Park, 7300 MacArthur Boulevard, Glen Echo, Maryland. Open daily. Admission to park free. Main (301) 492-6229, Recorded information (301) 492-6282, Adventure Theater (301) 320-5331, the Puppet Co. Playhouse (301) 320-6668

Goddard Space Flight Visitors Center, Soil Conservation Road, Greenbelt, Maryland. Open daily from 9 a.m. to 4 p.m. Call for tour schedule. Rocket launches the first and third Sundays of each month at 1 p.m. Admission free. (301) 286-8981

Great Falls and the Billy Goat Trail, See Chesapeake and Ohio Canal National Historical Park, Maryland.

Great Falls Park, end of Old Dominion Drive, Great Falls, Virginia. Open daily from 7:30 a.m. to dusk. Admission $2 per person or $4 per car. (703) 285-2965. www.nps.gov/gwmp.grfa

Hains Point, East Potomac Park, Ohio Drive, S.W. Golf course, (202) 554-7600. Tennis (202) 554-5962.

Hard Rock Café, 999 E Street, N.W. Metro stop: Metro Center. Open Sunday through Thursday from 11 a.m. to 11 p.m., Friday and Saturday from 11 a.m. to 1 a.m. (202) 737-7625

Hirshhorn Museum and Sculpture Garden, Independence Avenue and Seventh Street, S.W. Metro stop: L'Enfant Plaza. Open daily from 10 a.m. to 5:30 p.m. Sculpture garden open 7:30 a.m. to dusk. Admission free. (202) 357-2700. www.si.edu/organiza/museums/hirsh

Houston's Restaurant, 1065 Wisconsin Avenue, N.W. Open Monday through Thursday from 5 p.m. to 11 p.m.; Friday from 5 p.m. to midnight; Saturday from noon to midnight; Sunday from noon to 11 p.m. (202) 338-7760.

Jack's Boats, 3500 K Street, N.W. Call for hours and prices. (202) 337-9642

James Madison Memorial Building Cafeteria, 101 Independence Avenue, S.E. Metro stop: Capitol South. Open Monday through Saturday 9 a.m. to 11 a.m. and 12:30 p.m. to 3:30 p.m. (202) 707-8300

Jeepers, 700 Hungerford Drive, Rockville, Maryland, and 6041 Greenbelt Road, Greenbelt, Maryland. Open Monday through Thursday 11 a.m. to 8 p.m., Friday to 10 p.m., Saturday 10 a.m. to 10 p.m., and Sunday 11 a.m. to 8 p.m. Rockville (301) 309-2525, Greenbelt (301) 982-2444.

Jefferson Memorial, Tidal Basin, south end of 15th Street, S.W. Metro stop: Smithsonian or L'Enfant Plaza. Open daily from 8 a.m. to 11:45 p.m. Admission free. (202) 426-6841 or (202) 619-7222. www.nps.gov/thje

John F. Kennedy Center for the Performing Arts, 2700 F Street, N.W. Metro stop: Foggy Bottom/ George Washington University. Free tours. Information (202) 416-8340. Tickets (202) 467-4600 or (800) 444-1324. www.kennedy-center.org

Kenilworth Aquatic Gardens, Anacostia Avenue and Douglas Street, N.E. Metro stop: Deanwood. Open daily from 8 a.m.to 4 p.m. Admission free. (202) 426-6905

Korean War Veterans Memorial, south of Lincoln Memorial Reflecting Pool. Metro stop: Foggy Bottom/George Washington University. Open daily from 8 a.m. to 11:45 p.m. (202) 426-6841 or (202) 619-7222. www.nps.gov/kwvm

Library of Congress, 101 Independence Avenue, S.E. Metro stop: Capitol South. Call for hours. (202) 707-5000 or (202) 707-8000. www.loc.gov

Lincoln Memorial, West Potomac Park at 23rd Street, N.W. Metro stop: Foggy Bottom/George Washington University. Open daily from 8 a.m. to 11:45 p.m. (202) 426-6841 or (202) 619-7222. www.nps.gov/linc

Marrakesh, 617 New York Avenue, N.W. Metro stop: Gallery Place/Chinatown. Open from 6 p.m. to 11 p.m. Reservations required. (202) 393-9393

Mazza Gallerie, 5300 Wisconsin Avenue, N.W. Metro stop: Friendship Heights. Open daily. (202) 966-6114

MCI Center, 601 F Street, N.W. Metro stop: Gallery Place/ Chinatown. (202) 628-3200. MCI National Sports Gallery opens daily at noon. Admission $5, free for children under 5. (202) 661-5133. www.mcicenter.com

Mount Vernon, George Washington Parkway, Mount Vernon, Virginia. Open 8 a.m. to 5 p.m., April through August. Open 9 a.m. to 4 p.m., November through February, to 5 p.m. March, September, and October. Admission $8 adults, $4 children. (703) 780-2000. www.mountvernon.org

Music City Roadhouse, 1050 30th Street, N.W. Open Tuesday through Saturday from 4:30 p.m. to 10 p.m.; Sunday from 11 a.m. to 10 p.m. (202) 337-4444

National Air and Space Museum, Independence Avenue and Seventh Street, S.W. Metro stop: L'Enfant Plaza. Open daily from 10 a.m. to 5:30 p.m. Admission free. (202) 357-2700 or (202) 357-1400. www.nasm.si.edu

National Aquarium, U.S. Department of Commerce Building, 14th Street and Constitution Avenue, N.W. Metro stop: Federal Triangle or Metro Center. Open daily from 9 a.m. to 5 p.m. Admission $3 for adults, 75 cents for children under 12. Main (202) 482-2826, Recorded information (202) 482-2825

National Aquarium in Baltimore, Pier 3, 501 East Pratt Street, Baltimore, Maryland. Admission $14 for adults, $7.50 for children ages 3 through 11. Buy tickets by 3 p.m. on day of visit. Main (410) 576-3800, Advance tickets (800) 551-SEAT or (202) 432-SEAT. www.aqua.org

National Archives, Seventh Street and Pennsylvania Avenue, N.W. Metro stop: Archives/Navy Memorial. Open daily from 10 a.m. to 5:30 p.m. Open April 1 to Labor Day, daily from 10 a.m. to 9 p.m. Admission free. (202) 501-5000. www.nara.gov

National Gallery of Art, Fourth Street and Constitution Avenue, N.W. Metro stop: Archives/ Navy Memorial or Judiciary Square. Open Monday through Saturday from 10 a.m. to 5 p.m., Sunday from 11 a.m. to 6 p.m. Admission free. (202) 737-4215. www.nga.gov

National Gallery Cascade Café, Fourth Street and Constitution Avenue, N.W. Metro stop: Archives/ Navy Memorial or Judiciary Square. Open Monday through Saturday 10 a.m. to 4:30 p.m., Sunday 11 a.m. to 5:30 p.m. (202) 216-5966

National Gallery Sculpture Garden Ice Rink, Ninth Street and Constitution Avenue, N.W. Call for hours and skate rental prices. (202) 371-5340

National Mall, from the U.S. Capitol to the Washington Monument, and continuing east as Constitution Gardens to the Lincoln Memorial. Metro stop: Smithsonian. (202) 426-6841

National Museum of African Art, 950 Independence Avenue, S.W. Metro stop: Smithsonian. Open daily from 10 a.m. to 5:30 p.m. Admission free. (202) 357-4600. www.si.edu/ organiza/museums/africart

National Museum of American History, 14th Street and Constitution Avenue, N.W. Metro stop: Smithsonian or Federal Triangle. Open daily from 10 a.m. to 5:30 p.m. Admission free. (202) 357-2700. www.si.edu/nmah

National Museum of Natural History, Tenth Street and Constitution Avenue, N.W. Metro stop: Federal Triangle or Smithsonian. Open daily from 10 a.m. to

⇞ **The National Museum of Natural History**

5:30 p.m. Admission free. Main (202) 357-2700, Education office (202) 357-2066. www.nmnh.si.edu

National Museum of Women in the Arts, 1250 New York Avenue, N.W. Metro stop: Metro Center. Open Monday through Saturday from 10 a.m. to 5 p.m., Sunday from 12 noon to 5 p.m. Suggested donation of $3 for adults, $2 for children. (202) 783-5000. www.nmwa.org

National Theater, 1321 E Street, N.W. Free Saturday morning children's programs. (202) 783-3370

National Zoological Park (the National Zoo), 3001 Connecticut Avenue, N.W. Metro stop: Woodley

Park/Zoo. Admission free. Main (202) 673-4717, Concert series (202) 357-2700, Recorded information (202) 673-4800. www.si.edu/natzoo

Navy Museum, Building 76, Washington Navy Yard, 901 M Street, S.E. Metro stop: Eastern Market. Open weekdays 9 a.m. to 4 p.m., weekends, holidays, summer until 5 p.m. Admission free. (202) 433-4882

Newseum, Freedom Forum World Center, 1101 Wilson Boulevard, Arlington, Virginia. Metro stop: Rosslyn. Open Wednesday through Sunday, 10 a.m. to 5 p.m. Admission free. (888) NEWSEUM or (703) 284-3544. www.newseum.org

Oriole Park at Camden Yards, 333 Camden Street, Baltimore, Maryland. Orioles tickets $7 to $35. (410) 685-9800 or (410) 547-6234. www.theorioles.com

Oxon Hill Farm, 6411 Oxon Hill Road at I-495 Exit 3A, Oxon Hill, Maryland. Open daily from 9 a.m. to 5 p.m. Admission free. Main (301) 839-1177

Peirce Mill, Tilden Street and Beach Drive, N.W., in Rock Creek Park. Open Wednesday through Sunday from 9 a.m. to 5 p.m. Admission free. (202) 426-6908

Petersen House, 516 Tenth Street, N.W. Metro stop: Metro Center. Open daily from 9 a.m. to 5 p.m. Admission free. (202) 426-6924

Planet Hollywood, 1101 Pennsylvania Avenue,

N.W. Metro stop: Federal Triangle or Metro Center. Open daily 11 a.m. to 1 a.m. (202) 783-7827

Potomac Cannons, Pfitzner Stadium, off the Prince William Parkway, Woodbridge, Virginia. Admission $4.50 to $8.50. (703) 590-2311. www.potomaccannons.com

Potomac Mills, 2700 Potomac Mills Circle, off I-95, Exit 158B, Prince William, Virginia. Open Monday through Saturday from 10 a.m. to 9:30 p.m.; Sunday from 11 a.m. to 7 p.m. Phone (703) 643-1770 or (800) VA-MILLS. Call (703) 551-1050 for shuttle bus service. www.potomacmills.com

Red Sea, 2463 18th Street, N.W. Metro stop: Woodley Park/Zoo. Open daily from 11:45 a.m. to 11 p.m. (202) 483-5000

Reeves Restaurant & Bakery, 1306 G Street, N.W. Metro stop: Metro Center. Open Monday through Saturday from 7 a.m. to 6 p.m. (202) 628-6350

Robert F. Kennedy Memorial Stadium, 2400 East Capitol Street, S.E. Metro stop: Stadium/Armory. (202) 547-9077

Rock Creek Gallery, 2401 Tilden Street, in Rock Creek Park. Open Thursday through Sunday from 11 a.m. to 4 p.m. Closed in August. Admission free. (202) 244-2482

Rock Creek Nature Center and Planetarium, 5200 Glover Road, N.W. Open Wednesday through

Sunday 9 a.m. to 5 p.m. Call for speical programs. Admission free. (202) 426-6829

Rock Creek Park. Open daily until dusk. Admission to park free. Headquarters (202) 282-1063. Tennis reservations (202) 722-5949, picnic area reservations (202) 673-7646, golf (202) 882-7332. www.nps.gov/rocr

Rock Creek Park Horse Center, Military and Glover Roads, N.W. Call for hours and fees. Reservations (202) 362-0118, Recording (202) 362-0117

Samuel P. Langley IMAX Theater, National Air and Space Museum, Independence Avenue between Fourth and Seventh Streets. Metro stop: L'Enfant Plaza. Recorded information (202) 357-1686

Sherrill's Bakery, 233 Pennsylvania Avenue, S.E. Metro stop: Capitol South. Open Monday through Friday from 6 a.m. to 7 p.m., Saturday, Sunday, and holidays from 7 a.m. to 7 p.m. (202) 544-2480

Sholl's Colonial Cafeteria, 1990 K Street, N.W. Metro stop: Farragut West. Open Monday through Saturday from 7 a.m. to 10:30 a.m., 11 a.m. to 2:30 p.m., 4 p.m. to 8 p.m, Sunday from 8 a.m. to 3 p.m. (202) 296-3065

Shops at National Place, 529 14th Street, N.W. Metro stop: Metro Center. (202) 737-2379

Six Flags America, off Capital Beltway Exit 15A (Route 214 East), Largo, Maryland. Metro stop: Addison Road, transfer to Six Flags bus. Call for hours. Admission $31.99 for adults, $15.99 for children 48 inches and shorter, free for children under 3. Parking is $7 per car. (301) 249-1500. www.sixflags.com/america

Smithsonian Information Center, (202) 357-2700 or TTY (202) 357-1729

Supreme Court of the United States, First Street and Maryland Avenue, N.E. Metro: Union Station or Capitol South. Admission free. (202) 479-3000. Supreme Court Cafeteria, open Monday through Friday from 7:30 a.m. to 2 p.m. (with periodic closings). (202) 479-3246

Theodore Roosevelt Island, off the northbound lanes of George Washington Memorial Parkway on Virginia side of Potomac River. Open daily from 8 a.m. to dusk. Admission free. (703) 289-2550. www.nps.gov/this

Thompson's Boat Center, Virginia Avenue and Rock Creek Parkway, Georgetown. Call for hours and prices. (202) 333-9543

Tidal Basin Boat House, 1501 Maine Avenue, S.W. Metro stop: Smithsonian or L'Enfant Plaza. Opens daily at 10 a.m., March through October. Hourly rentals are $7 for a two-person pedal boat, $14 for a four-person boat. (202) 479-2426

Torpedo Factory Art Center, 105 North Union Street, Alexandria, Virginia. Open daily from 10 a.m. to 5 p.m. Admission free. (703) 838-4565. www.torpedofactory.org

Union Station, 40 Massachusetts Avenue, N.E. Metro stop: Union Station. Open daily. Stores open Monday through Saturday from 10 a.m. to 9 p.m., Sunday from 12 noon to 6 p.m. Call for movie and restaurant information. (202) 289-1908

United States Botanic Garden, Maryland Avenue and First Street, S.W. Metro stop: Federal Center Southwest. Open daily from 9 a.m. to 5 p.m. Closed during 2000 for major renovation. Admission free. (202) 225-8333. www.aoc.gov/usbg

United States Capitol, Capitol Hill. Metro stop: Union Station or Capitol South. Open daily September through February 9 a.m. to 4:30 p.m. March through August open 8 a.m. to 8 p.m. Daily tours start every 10-15 minutes in Rotunda from 9 a.m. to 3:45 p.m. When Congress is in session, get passes to visit the Senate or House of Representatives gallery from your senator's or representative's office. Admission free. Guide service (202) 225-6827, Capitol switchboard (202) 224-3121. www.aoc.gov, www.senate.gov, www.house.gov

United States Holocaust Memorial Museum, 100 Raoul Wallenberg Place, S.W. Metro stop: Smithsonian. Open daily 10 a.m. to 5:30 p.m. Admission free, but timed entry passes required. Daily pass distribution begins at 10 a.m. Advance tickets obtained for a service charge from PROTIX at (800) 400-9373. (202) 833-6060. www.ushmm.org

United States National Arboretum, 3501 New York Avenue, N.E. Open daily from 8 a.m. to 5 p.m. National Bonsai and Penjing Museum open daily from 10 a.m. to 3:30 p.m. Admission free. (202) 245-2726. www.ars-grin.gov

United States Navy Memorial and Naval Heritage Center, 701 Pennsylvania Avenue, N.W. Metro stop: Archives/Navy Memorial. Memorial open daily, 24 hours. Naval Heritage Center open Monday through Saturday from 9:30 a.m. to 5 p.m., Sunday from noon to 5 p.m. (202) 737-2300

Vietnam Veterans Memorial, Constitution Gardens, at Constitution Avenue and Henry Bacon Drive, N.W. Metro stop: Foggy Bottom/George Washington University. Open daily, 8 a.m. to 11:45 p.m. Admission free. (202) 426-6841 or (202) 619-7222

Vietnam Women's Memorial, Constitution Gardens, at 21st Street. Metro stop: Foggy Bottom/ George Washington University. Open daily, 8 a.m. to 11:45 p.m. Admission free. (202) 426-6841 or (202) 619-7222

Washington Capitals, MCI Center, 601 F Street, N.W. Metro stop: Gallery Place/Chinatown. Admission $10 and up. (202) 661-5050 or (202) 432-SEAT for individual tickets. www.washingtoncaps.com

Washington Monument, 15th Street and Constitution Avenue, N.W. Metro stop: Smithsonian. Get timed passes at the kiosk at the foot at monument. Open daily from 8 a.m. to 4:45 p.m., April through Labor Day open 8 a.m. to 11:45 p.m. Admission free. (202) 426-6841 or (202) 619-7222. www.nps.gov/wamo

Washington National Cathedral, Massachusetts and Wisconsin Avenue, N.W. Open daily from 10 a.m. to 4:30 p.m. Free admission. Main (202) 537-6200, www.cathedral.org

Washington Redskins, FedEx Field, Landover, Maryland. (301) 276-6060

Washington Wizards, MCI Center, 601 F Street, N.W. Metro stop: Gallery Place/Chinatown. Call

for ticket prices. (202) 661-5050 or (202) 432-SEAT for individual tickets. www.nba.com/wizards

White House, 1600 Pennsylvania Avenue, N.W. Metro: Federal Triangle or McPherson Square. Open for tours Tuesday through Saturday from 10 a.m. to 12 noon. Free same-day timed tickets are required from March through Labor Day and in December. Get them starting at 7:30 a.m. at the White House Visitor Center, 1450 Pennsylvania Avenue, N.W. Information line (202) 456-2200, White House Visitor Center (202) 208-1631. www.whitehouse.gov

Wright Place, National Air and Space Museum, Independence Avenue and Seventh Street, S. W. Metro stop: L'Enfant Plaza. Cafe open daily 11:30 a.m. to 3 p.m., 11 a.m. to 4 p.m. in summer. (202) 357-2700

Zed's Ethiopian Cuisine, 1201 28th Street, N.W. Open daily from 11 a.m. to 11 p.m. (202) 333-4710

ANSWERS TO PUZZLES

page 11

page 13

K O N I T K M J S O P M Y P V U H
D P H F N D Q S U M H E B P O N H
O Y L L S V A I N D P T S O L T P
C T P I D R E K A T G N G S L U R
T A L W B M N S T U D E N T E D E
O E A E M R F N T N N O G M Y E S
R D W R G U A N H I I U Y A B W I
S A Y S P C I R D K G L M N A D D
P S E N A T O R I B O A T F L Q E
U I R E I S U R N A Y D T L L U N
R O T B L K I T E U N I M O N F T
D A M B A S S A D O R S B E R Q R

page 19

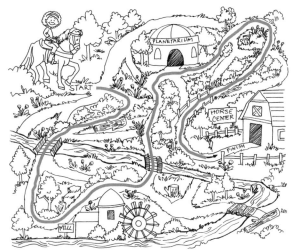

page 21

page 25

page 27

```
R O T A T H I K E O P S W I N G S
H P C E R D Q S Y M H E S A O N H
G W G L N G A I N N T T C B L T F
P T S O D N S K A A I N U F L U D
R O A W G M I R K V C E L T I D N
S F N E M D F S G N N O P T Y S Y
P I D S D G U N N C U I U T E B W H
I A X S S C I N D O C L U R A D W
C Y B I K E P A T H U A R U N Q T
N I A R T S D L N P Y R E M O I B
I O T B B I R D S U L I T R E E S
C P D N I O P Y F K J Z H S E Q R
```

page 29

page 35

page 39

¹S	H	²E	A	R		³H
		L				O
⁴F	E	E	D	I	N	G
		P				S
		H				
⁵R	A	B	B	I	⁶T	
		N			O	
		T		⁷C	O	W	S
					L	
	⁸F	A	R	M	S	

page 41

page 43

page 49

page 53

page 55

	¹P	R	E	²S	I	D	E	N	³T	
	L			T					H	
⁴A	B	R	A	H	A	M	⁵M		E	
	Y			T			A		A	
		⁶C		U			R		T	
⁷L	I	F	E				Y		E	
		V							R	
		I								
⁸S	L	A	V	E	R	Y				

page 67

page 69

```
F P I T C H E R S O P M B A S E S
B T C J K D Q S Y M D E M N O N L
N M A S C O T I N L P T S B L T F
S T T O D R S P E A N U T S L U X
U K C F G M N I D U C E N T E D F
M L H N M D F N R N N O G T Y G H
P D E M G T N E H U I U Y E B L J
I O R F U V M N D K F L M R A O F
R P I O U O R O W B C A H F Q V G
E I Z C H S U R N P Y D N L L E B
G N F D L K I T I C K E T S N F S
V C O A C H P Y F R I X B E L Q R
```

page 71

page 79

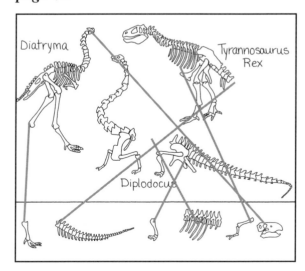

page 83

page 85

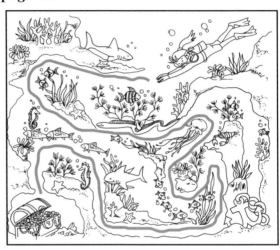

page 87

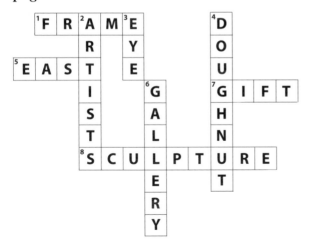

page 89

page 95

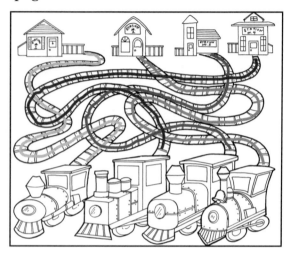

page 97

page 99

```
B D L V T S T A G E P M Y P V U A
M J T R U M P E T M H E B A O N S
I Z H X S O M U S I C S T A N D D
C J F Z B R S K B X I N G U I N M
R K T A G A N R D V C E N T I V U
O U U Q M D T N G N N O G L Y E S
P D I W G U N O H U I U O E B W I
H S D R U M I K N K C I M R A D C
O L P R J K R O W B V A T F L Q I
N H L T I W U R N P Y D N L L U A
E V M C O N D U C T O R M Y N F N
A W S B I O P Y F R I C L E E Q R
```

page 101

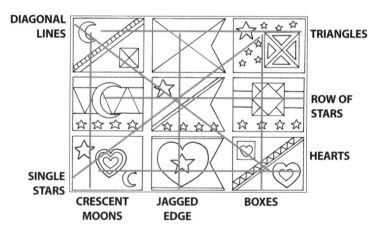

DIAGONAL LINES

TRIANGLES

ROW OF STARS

HEARTS

SINGLE STARS

CRESCENT MOONS

JAGGED EDGE

BOXES

page 107

Answer: a crab

page 109

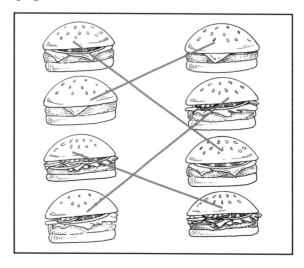

page 111

GEOGRAPHICAL INDEX: WHERE IS EVERYTHING?

INDEX

Guidebooks that really *guide*

City•Smart™ Guidebooks

Pick one for your favorite city: *Albuquerque, Anchorage, Austin, Calgary, Charlotte, Chicago, Cincinnati, Cleveland, Denver, Indianapolis, Kansas City, Memphis, Milwaukee, Minneapolis/St. Paul, Nashville, Pittsburgh, Portland, Richmond, Salt Lake City, San Antonio, San Francisco, St. Louis, Tampa/St. Petersburg, Tucson.* US $12.95 to 15.95

Retirement & Relocation Guidebooks

The World's Top Retirement Havens, Live Well in Honduras, Live Well in Ireland, Live Well in Mexico. US $15.95 to $16.95

Travel•Smart® Guidebooks

Trip planners with select recommendations to *Alaska, American Southwest, Arizona, Carolinas, Colorado, Deep South, Eastern Canada, Florida, Florida Gulf Coast, Hawaii, Illinois/Indiana, Kentucky/Tennessee, Maryland/Delaware, Michigan, Minnesota/Wisconsin, Montana/Wyoming/Idaho, New England, New Mexico, New York State, Northern California, Ohio, Pacific Northwest, Pennsylvania/New Jersey, South Florida and the Keys, Southern California, Texas, Utah, Virginias, Western Canada.* US $14.95 to $17.95

Rick Steves' Guides

See *Europe Through the Back Door* and take along guides to *France, Belgium & the Netherlands; Germany, Austria & Switzerland; Great Britain & Ireland; Italy; Scandinavia; Spain & Portugal; London; Paris;* or *Best of Europe.* US $12.95 to $21.95

Adventures in Nature

Plan your next adventure in *Alaska, Belize, Caribbean, Costa Rica, Guatemala, Hawaii, Honduras, Mexico.* US $17.95 to $18.95

Into the Heart of Jerusalem

A traveler's guide to visits, celebrations, and sojourns. US $17.95

The People's Guide to Mexico

This is so much more than a guidebook—it's a trip to Mexico in and of itself, complete with the flavor of the country and its sights, sounds, and people. US $22.95

JOHN MUIR PUBLICATIONS
A DIVISION OF AVALON TRAVEL PUBLISHING
5855 Beaudry Street, Emeryville, CA 94608

Please check our web site at www.travelmatters.com for current prices and editions, or see your local bookseller.